It Only Gets Better FROM HERE

A JOURNEY FROM FEAR TO TRUST

JOANNE MITCHELL

It Only Gets Better from Here

Copyright © 2024 Joanne Mitchell

All rights reserved. No part of this publication may be reproduced, distributed, or transmitted in any form or by any means, including photocopying, recording, or other electronic or mechanical methods, without the prior written permission of the copyright holder, except in the case of brief quotations embodied in critical reviews and certain other noncommercial uses permitted by copyright law.

Book Design by
Transcendent Publishing

ISBN: 979-8-9906867-7-9

Printed in the United States of America.

I dedicate this book to my two beautiful daughters, who gave me the incentive to thrive and make me proud every day.

TABLE OF CONTENTS

Introduction vii

Chapter 1 – Imagination 1

Chapter 2 – Inheritance: The Story Behind the Story 5

Chapter 3 – Not Good Enough 13

Chapter 4 – The Big Bang 17

Chapter 5 – Gender Difference (Early Working Years) 23

Chapter 6 – 'Til Death Do Us Part 29

Chapter 7 – Pregnancy and Childbirth .33

Chapter 8 – Happy Families 39

Chapter 9 – Back to Work & Life Lessons 43

Chapter 10 – End Date 49

Chapter 11 – History Repeats Itself 55

Chapter 12 – Lock the Doors 61

Chapter 13 – DIY 69

Chapter 14 – Self-Worth 75

Chapter 15 – Control 79

Chapter 16 – Self-Love...85
Chapter 17 – Connected 91
Chapter 18 – The Great Awakening..........................99
Chapter 19 – Purpose..105
Chapter 20 – Grace 111
Chapter 21 – Passing on..117
Chapter 22 – The End is the Beginning 127

Bibliography..135
Acknowledgments 137
Stay Connected 139
About the Author..141

INTRODUCTION

*"Life can only be understood backwards;
but it must be lived forwards."*

~ Soren Kierkegaard

I am writing this book as an act of courage, daring to show up as my authentic self and trusting that I will attract to me all that I am. There is no time to play small and, as the saying goes, "nothing to fear but fear itself." As I share my path – a winding road of anxiety, struggle, happiness, joy, and tears – I hope you see your own story as perfect and know you are not alone. I am still, and always will be, a work in progress, but I hope to leave something for my children that shows I keep striving to be my best self.

I wrote this book as if singing a song from my heart, all the while looking around to see who would be tapping their feet to the music. They are my tribe. I would describe myself as many things; however, a writer is not one of them. I simply wrote as though we were relaxing together, contemplating our lives and what we have in common. My hope is that it helps every woman who feels there is something more within her to be discovered.

Each of us, regardless of age or life success, reaches a point when we just know there must be "something else" in life. I have been at this point, and I know that, though it feels uncomfortable, it is actually the start of awakening to a new relationship with yourself and with life itself. This journey took me from striving to survive to thriving as the most passionate, best self possible. It also resulted in my caring less about what other people think about me – and I hope it does the same for you.

The most incredible excitement awaits in the unknown. Is this your grand call to be pulled out of an outdated "normal" life and leave previously known limits behind? How can you explore while feeling safe and held? My story is not your story, as you are unique and perfect as you are. The opportunity is simply to start undertaking the challenge, to go within and know yourself. In shining a light on myself, my intent is to help you shed light on any darkness or lack of clarity about your future. Not to fix or show you the way, but to enable you to see your options more clearly. Everything I have learned along the journey has been one of gaining perspective and practicing loving awareness.

Should you listen to me? No; that would be letting go of your intuition. Just read a story and feel what resonates and holds meaning or value in your life.

The themes in this book are relationships, belonging, worth, and perspective. All the formal education that allowed me a thirty-five-year career as an IT professional taught me nothing about the essence of life. Learning to surrender while taking 100% responsibility for my life and putting my heart in the driver's seat – that seems to have been gathered along the way.

Our bodies are organizations of organisms. We can dissect something to see its mechanism, but it will not help us know its essence. The work of a sharp mind is to cut things up to understand them. The physical brain is indeed two halves, while the heart is one.

Looking back, I can see that all the significant changes and growth in my life happened in times of challenge. A comfort zone seems safe, but we are only assimilating our past experiences, not breaking new ground toward self-realization. We have all heard of growing pains, and I feel this truth in my lived experience. Next time you experience challenging things in your life, whatever they may be, take a moment to breathe and say to yourself, "Here I grow again!"

Life does not suddenly become perfect. In releasing all the "sticky stuff" that no longer serves me, I have found most progress comes from my training as a life-force artist, coach, and Qigong practitioner, rather than my higher education. Now I have enough grey hair and just enough wisdom to know the foolish game I have been playing. While I have something to protect, there is still fear within me. Where there is fear, there are boundaries created to keep me safe. How can I stretch to new limitless possibilities if I live in a secure box of my own making? These days, I am grateful for every opportunity I get to ferret out all these old beliefs and stories so I can clear them.

For sure, we will never be free of challenges. They are part of life. There will always be so much that is not in my control: wars, famine, pandemics, illness, and death. The list goes on and on, but I can consistently challenge my response because this is *always* in my control. I can choose how I feel. It is okay to be angry or sad, but knowing it's my choice allows me to stay with that emotional experience only as long as I need to. I can't observe my reaction without stepping back, and this act of separation changes my relationship with it. The eye can't see itself. I become the observer and the creator of my life story. There will still be bumps in the road, and I may still get hurt, but there is just a little more space to start remembering who I truly am.

The more I practice keeping my heart open even when it hurts, the greater my chance of being a heart-centered, present person. I don't have to run and hide when things get uncomfortable. I choose to be less filled with the importance of what I imagine I should be doing in the world. I prefer to awaken to grace and unconditional love. I want to laugh more, to dance and play. I am so grateful for everything, especially for you, dear reader.

Each chapter contains a story that raises questions to spark awareness of how we choose to live. From this perspective, I reflect on the life lesson, what it meant to me, and what we might learn together. Accept the invitation to contemplate your life story, discover its treasures, and trust the wisdom that waits in your heart.

I promise you won't be the same person after reading this book. While you will not, of course, be a completely new person, there is no doubt you are constantly changing. Your body is creating millions of new cells every minute. Greek philosopher Heraclitus said you could not step into the same river twice because you and the river have changed. If you can connect to your heart, open your mind, take the time to be still, and listen to the wise self within, you will discover how to create a new life experience, consciously.

May your life be a thrilling, page-turning adventure with growth and experiences beyond your wildest dreams.

"Pain pushes, until vision pulls."

~ Michael Bernard Beckwith

This is the story of my life.

Here is a fun exercise: Imagine you were going to make a movie about your life and family. Now, choose the actors that will play the leading roles.

I did this with my own family before writing this book. We laughed a lot as we saw the difference between the actor each of us chose for ourselves and those chosen by other family members. I guess this is an exercise in self-perception. We looked at both old and young versions and even found some pictures of the actors together! It was not simply about what they looked like but feeling into the character they needed to portray. I share my choices with you to set the scene as we begin the story together.

My mother – Shirley MacLaine
My father – Michael Caine
My husband – Michael Gross, from *Family Ties*.
Me – Jane Fonda (wishful thinking, maybe)

CHAPTER 1

IMAGINATION

*"True imagination is not fanciful dreaming;
it is fire from heaven."*

~ Ernst Holmes

1970

I can't see his face, just the whites of his eyes and a flash of his teeth, as he peers through the window of my room. It is dark and, absolutely frozen, I don't move until he moves away. I must find somewhere to hide before he breaks in. I struggle to think clearly; every room in the house has a window; the bathroom window is small, but there's no lock on the door! The linen cupboard is my best option, and I manage to squeeze in underneath the bottom shelf; quietly pulling the door closed, I wait, barely breathing. There is the sound of smashing glass. He must be inside. My heart is beating loudly, and I'm sure he will hear me. I listen to him going through the house and his footsteps approaching. The door is yanked open, and he reaches in to grab me. I open my mouth to scream but make no sound.

I wake up. My heart is still pounding and my body is drenched in sweat. I lay there in the dark, terrified to go back to sleep. I dread nighttime; everything scares me when I can't see clearly. Swallowing my pride, I creep into my little brother's room; beside him in bed, I feel safe. He is fast asleep, and I don't disturb him. Hopefully, I can return to my bed before he wakes when it gets light.

I'd always had nightmares; my parents didn't take kindly to being woken up and sent me back to my room. I was always so grateful when the dawn broke; the light made everything feel normal and safe again. I stood accused of having an overactive imagination, and my "'tend friends," as my parents called them, were not allowed to stay. My mother put them ceremoniously in the bin – a big upset in my little life as they were indeed friends and very real to me. It was time to grow up. My father was my hero, and I learned quickly that the game of life was to be a good girl. Daddy liked good girls, and I tried hard not to disappoint him. I did not understand that all those rules were for my own good. My parents wanted me to grow up freely, without being judged by class. I learned the rules quickly, how to talk politely, eat correctly, and dress appropriately. Of course, we had to eat all the food on our plates. "There are starving children in the world, and you are lucky to not be one of them." How would stuffing more food, which I did not like or want, into my tummy possibly benefit other hungry children? I sat through many a meal with tears plopping into a plate of cold spinach.

My brother once caught our mother harvesting greens from the vegetable patch and exclaimed, "I knew it; you've been feeding us weeds!" That more or less sums up our appreciation of healthy, homegrown food, and eating it felt like torture. Being taught table manners at home ensured we would not be an embarrassment to our parents when we ate out in public. Sometimes, when there had been some misdemeanor (i.e., talking with one's mouthful or putting elbows on the table), my father would thump on the table so hard the cutlery and crockery would temporarily levitate before crashing back down.

During dinner one evening, my little brother, enjoying his food, burped loudly.

"Excuse me!" my father snapped, incensed at this breach of decorum.

My brother looked up from his plate and innocently said, "You may leave the table."

Even Dad had to laugh at that.

For all the rules and discipline, I knew my parents loved me. I also discovered a love for stories, as my mother read to us at bedtime. My favorite book was *The Magic Faraway Tree* by Enid Blyton, where each character had a unique voice and I could imagine each scene like it was real.

I adored my little brother; the five-year difference was just enough for me to feel able to protect him. Whatever happened in our lives, we had each other. I grew up knowing I belonged in this family nucleus; I built protective walls around it in my mind. While the outside world was scary, here, I felt safe. I luckily experienced the most important formative years of my life on a solid foundation.

We are born with two fears, loud noises and falling; everything else we learn. The most profound thing we realize is our dependency on others, leading to our fear of abandonment. Connection is almost on the same survival level as food and water. We need each other to survive and prosper.

Happy people are loosely attached to life. Fear is simply an overactive imagination since we can only fear what has not yet happened. We can't manage fear because it is trying to control a consequence; we must look at the cause. Imagination is a powerful force of creation, calling forth your latent powers, talents, and abilities. While the soul creates, the mind reacts. Look closely at the words reactive and creative. Just the "c" in a different position, and we can all choose how we "see" things.

> *"Logic will get you from A to B, imagination will take you everywhere."*
>
> ~ Einstein

Do you still have fears limiting how fully you live your life?

Did you build walls to protect yourself when you did not feel safe?

Do you still have an active imagination, or did you lock it away when you grew up?

CHAPTER 2

INHERITANCE: THE STORY BEHIND THE STORY

"Remember that everyone you meet is afraid of something, loves something and has lost something."

~ H. Jackson Brown Jr.

1940

*D*o you remember how your great-great-great grandparents looked? If not, look in the mirror, as their nose is on your face!

London, England

My paternal grandfather was born in 1910, followed by a younger brother and sister. He got married when he was just twenty-one years old. He started as a draftsman and later became a chief aircraft designer; this was declared a reserved job in England, so he was not drafted to fight in World War II. Born in 1907, my grandmother was a few years older than him and from a very different background. Her family was in the fur trade, making coats, and though this was lucrative, money was often tight because there were seven children – five girls and two boys – to feed. At age twenty-four she married my grandfather and they had one daughter and two boys, my father, born in 1939, being the youngest. By all accounts, they had a close, loving family. My grandfather could cook and even do dressmaking, though he always got a cake baked for him on his birthday.

In November 1940, when my dad was just eighteen months old, the Germans bombed their home. Like many families in England at that time, my grandparents had an Anderson shelter at the end of their garden to protect them in the event of an air raid – one of millions of such shelters distributed by The Ministry of Home Security. These small, corrugated steel structures, which homeowners could erect, partially dig into the ground, and cover with earth, were designed to withstand the blast from a nearby bomb. Despite these efforts, the Germans' strategic bombing of the UK between 1939 and 1945 would destroy 220,000 dwellings and kill around 50,000 people!

My Auntie Pam, who was eight years old at the time, told me the story. They had chosen not to sleep in the shelter that night because my father had bronchitis and it would have been too cold and damp for him. Instead, my grandfather rearranged the furniture in the front room so they could all sleep together.

Pam awoke to the explosion, sat up, and saw that the outside wall of the room had been blown away. Across the road was a blazing fire where their neighbors' home once stood. It had taken a direct hit and was reduced to a pile of rubble, the couple inside killed instantly. Air raid wardens with a station in the road were also all killed that night.

Her mother told Pam to put on her boots and coat; she would return to collect her as soon as they had her younger brothers safely out to the shelter. Pam clearly remembered the glass on the floor cutting her feet as she tried to find the boots; she also recalled not being afraid because of the immense love in the family. They spent the rest of the night in the shelter and, aside from her mom, who was injured when a brick landed on her head, were remarkably unharmed. A door blasted across the arms of a wooden chair that folded out to a single bed, saving my uncle, who was sleeping in it. A blanket pulled tight over the top of my father's cot kept him safe as debris and bits of glass landed on top of it.

This happy family survived the war years, never imagining that a far more significant trauma lay around the corner. When my aunt was sixteen and training to be a nursery nurse, she returned home to find her mother in bed with a splitting headache. They only had aspirin, but she could not even keep that down, and they called the family doctor, who came directly after performing a surgery. He said she might have had an infection, but when he returned the next day they called an ambulance to take her to the hospital. She urgently needed an operation to remove a brain tumor they had discovered.

That evening, my aunt answered the ringing phone to hear the senior nurse at the hospital on the other end. When she asked about her mother's condition, she got the unimaginable news – her mother had died during the surgery! Her father had not made it to the hospital from work, and her brothers had not even had a chance to see her before she left home. Their entire world had capsized. My aunt took on the role of mother to the boys and tried to support her father as best she could, doing all the housework and laundry. She was ironing twenty-one shirts a week – unimaginable for someone like me, who owns very few items that need ironing. My grandfather did remarry, and in 1953 their son was born. Quite a strange coincidence that my grandfather, like his first wife, also had a brain tumor and died in 1975, but I at least got to know him. I remember visiting him in the hospital when he was having radium therapy. The tumor had paralyzed him on the right side so I had to stand on his left to hold his hand and talk to him.

On my mother's side, it was the opposite: I never knew my grandfather, who died in 1949 when she was only nine years old. Oddly enough, that was the same year my father, then age ten, lost his mother.

I had a special relationship with my maternal grandmother, whom I called Nana Gee. Born in 1901, she was also a young mother during the

War. In fact, my mother was born on September 3, 1940, the first day of the massive bombings on London. On September 7, three hundred German bombers began an onslaught that would last fifty-seven consecutive nights. What a time to have a new baby! What kind of world would she grow up in?

I was born in South Africa, and I live in England. My parents were born in England and lived in South Africa. I found this interesting and had fun looking at the different perspectives these lives revealed.

My mother met my father, a young toolmaker apprentice, and they were married in 1960. They immigrated to South Africa in 1963, arriving on April Fools' Day.

According to my mother, it had been a horrible winter in England and my father's psoriasis meant he had to spend long hours under a UV lamp. They were longing for some sun and adventure, and the four-year contract my father had signed up for in South Africa promised both. They knew little about the country and were looking forward to a different life. They were so courageous to take this giant leap into the unknown, though of course it was a massive shock for their families. My grandmother imagined Africa as a land of heathens, and my father's sister was heartbroken to see them go, as she thought she would never see them again!

At first – especially while they waited long, long weeks for their belongings to arrive – my mother was very lonely. She remembers looking in a shop window one day, hearing a child call out "Auntie," and thinking it was her nephew – though of course that was impossible. Later, she learned that well-brought-up Afrikaans children call all ladies "Auntie" or "Tannie."

They bought a car, she got a job, and they had their first magical trip to the Kruger National Park, one of the largest game reserves in Africa, covering 19,485 km². It was supposedly the best time to visit Kruger – back when it was all dirt roads and the camps had only little rondavels with shared cooking huts. It is much more modern today, but, as I can attest, still quite magical.

Once their belongings arrived, they rented a place with a garden and things improved. They never ceased to marvel at the beautiful sunshine.

Imagine, the washing would dry before my mother finished hanging it on the line!

They also enjoyed many other aspects of the lifestyle there, which was a vast improvement and streaks ahead of what they had known in England. In one of her weekly letters home, Mom told Nana Gee that their rented house was so big you could run a bus service from the front door to the kitchen!

By the time I came along in 1964, my parents realized that they were making it harder and harder to leave South Africa. They had their own house by then, and though my mother didn't have her own car she did have a bicycle with a wicker seat on the back for me. (According to Mom, I loved it.) And life became much easier when my mother's only brother and sister-in-law came from England with their two children. I was too young to remember, but Mom told me that we had great holidays with them and saw much of the country. However, while she felt less isolated, their mother was now alone in England, without her children and grandchildren. For Nana Gee, another continent may as well have been another planet.

Looking at it through adult eyes, I can see how incredibly sad that must have been for her. My grandmother would never have wanted to live in South Africa as she disliked the heat. My parents were happy to pay for her airfare to visit us anytime, but she only came a few times. It was too hard to say goodbye, she said. I never understood why she would miss the pleasure of seeing us in person because it would come to an end; again, I now see things from a different perspective.

How she must have lived for Mom's weekly letters! When sorting out her possessions after she died in 1979, they discovered that Nana Gee had kept each and every one. How can I complain, when nowadays we can chat anywhere in the world without cost and get pictures in an instant? My grandmother used to post her local newspapers, *The Enfield Gazette* and *The Observer* every week, rolling them up tight with a small piece of brown paper labeled "printed matter." I remember receiving these, and when we opened the pages, very often, some surprise from Nana Gee was hiding inside.

"Any Dream Will Do" was my grandmother's favorite song from the play J*oseph and the Amazing Technicolor Dream Coat.* One year, all four grandchildren sang this song, recorded on a cassette tape, and sent it to her in England. I am sure no one thought how sad that might make her as she listened to it alone, and so far away.

Of course, my paternal grandfather missed us terribly too. I got this most precious gift – a note, written by him – from my cousin in England.

<u>*To Joanne Louise on the occasion of her Christening*</u>

Far away in a distant land, on Sunday, so I understand,
A little girl in silk and lace, so dimpled and so fair of face;
is to be named, Joanne Louise, two pretty names,
so sure too please.
On Sunday, though you're far away,
my thoughts will be with you all day.
Your hair, the colour of your eyes, these things I have to visualise.
Because, of course, I have not seen a picture, of my beauty queen.
And when you come home, in a while,
I'll hear you laugh and see your smile.
By then, you will have reached your threes –
But you'll still be Joanne Louise.

Grandpa, 3 Feb 1965

This poem is so beautiful and sweet, it touched me beyond words. I have no idea where it had been for fifty-five years, and when I asked my mother she said she did not even know it existed. Maybe it's as simple as my grandfather forgetting to put it in the post?

With all my grandchildren living on different continents, I can better understand how my grandparents felt. Yes, as mentioned earlier, we can stay connected with our loved ones remotely. We can follow their lives; if they are happy and doing well, all is fine. It is only after we see them again after some time, get to hug them, and look into their eyes, that we realize what we were missing. What we pretended was okay and enough, was not. When we separate again, they leave a gaping hole; we feel their absence intensely. Saying goodbye is always painful, but it's even worse if we do not know when we will be able to see each other again.

Air travel is fantastic, but I never took crossing a border for granted. It is unnatural for families to be separated, but ours has been, for generations. My mother now refers to us as the "Scatterlings of Africa" (a great song by Johnny Clegg and Savuka (1987)). I know we are not unique, that there have always been families divided by war or other life circumstances, but I still wish we could enjoy ours without flying around the world.

I love how Julia Cameron, in her book *The Artist's Way*, uses her grandmother's struggles as an example of how we can best interact with the life we are given. "My grandmother knew what a painful life had taught her," Cameron wrote, "success or failure, the truth of life really has little to do with quality. The quality of life is always in proportion to the capacity for delight. The capacity for delight is the gift of paying attention …." She also described letters from her grandmother as the "flora and fauna reports."

My mother's emails, in which she delivers the weekend news to her children and grown-up grandchildren, are much the same. They're a very intimate view into her life. I always know what veggies she's harvested and what she did with them; I know what birds were in the garden, and when they were nesting, I learned who was sick and who was well. This little excerpt might give you a better idea:

> I love having a birthday in the spring, just wish you could see my garden now. Not only is the jasmine smelling gorgeous, but the wisteria is now rampaging all over the carport and adding to the delightful fragrance in the kitchen. I am picking some broad beans, plus some asparagus every evening for my supper. Garden birds are in glorious mating plumage and making the most of the things put out for them to eat. Let me tell you, I have been surprised by the many species that go for the bonemeal I get from the butcher, even sparrows… seems not many are vegetarians!

I have a wonderful family. Honestly, I look at each one with admiration. I love knowing that I carry my ancestors' genes and that my grandparents live within me at a cellular level. When I feel like nothing special, I look to my family with pride and know there must be something of worth within me too. This family is the foundation of my life.

A long life does not necessarily equal a good life, and a good one does not need to last into old age. Your life is your message to the world; is it inspiring? The word inspire is the act of taking a breath of air. Inspiration is also "in Spirit" and in enjoyment. Your breath is in the present moment. Is there a sense of quality in what you do? Even the most straightforward action requires your presence and full attention. Life is a string of present moments put together. Time is now, so live today.

Decide how many years you would still like to live. Do the math; how many weekends and days do you have left? When we do this little exercise, it reminds us how precious time is; it's our limited resource. Maybe we're the ones moving, not time, but we feel the movement all the same. Identifying with the inner part of ourselves that does *not* get old – rather than the body that changes through the ages and stages of our lives – is the secret to aging exquisitely.

> "The illusion of time will give way to the reality of time … and time present is made before time becomes present. For all time is here, now, in our awakening."
>
> ~ Ben Okri

CHAPTER 3

NOT GOOD ENOUGH

"It's not what you don't know that hurts you, but what you know for sure that just ain't so."

~ Mark Twain

1976

It is an average afternoon: I come home from school, get out of my school uniform, and eat lunch as quickly as possible so I can finish my homework and go outside. The sun is shining, and I am eager to jump into the pool to cool down. Today is different in one respect: I have a knot in my stomach because I must show my father my school report when he gets home from work. I am pretty happy with it but I know he won't be, and that is weighing heavy on my heart as I go for a swim. When it's time I get out and dry, carefully selecting my clothes, hoping that looking good might distract him from too harsh a judgment of my performance. Hearing him come through the door, I give him time to talk to my mother about his day and relax before gathering the courage to enter the lounge, report in hand. I had achieved sixty percent overall – above the fifty-one-percent class average – but he is unimpressed. "Forget all the other kids," he says, "If they are equally stupid, it is not going to help you. When you are looking for work and know only sixty percent, that means there is another forty percent you do not know how to do! Who in their right mind would hire you? If you do not learn to raise your standards, you will end up unemployed and on the streets!"

Even more critical than the marks were the teachers' comments. My math teacher wrote, "She could do better if she paid attention" – damming evidence that I was not just stupid but lazy, and there was no excuse for not doing your best! Even though my father never raised his voice; I knew he was disappointed, which hurt much more.

This is indeed a dog-eat-dog world, and only the fittest survive. I mastered the art of somehow passing the exams at school. I have Dad to thank for my strong work ethic. My mother, on the other hand, would often quote this famous adage: "If you say nothing, people might think you stupid; if you open your mouth, you will leave them in no doubt." I had a little autograph book and asked friends and family to write something to me on each page. The cute norm for these notes is, "When on this page you looked, and on this page you found. You will remember the one who spoiled the book by writing upside down." My Aunt Joan, however, wrote, "For those that talk and talk, this proverb may appeal; the steam that blows the whistle will never turn the wheel." Between them, I understood that I was not very smart and had little of value to talk about; only hard work would save me.

At 11 years old, I was afforded a private education at an all-girls senior school. My parents made this major decision and investment, and I knew I should be grateful. Having attended a local co-ed primary school, this was a significant change for me. I was a "day scholar" and spent forty-five minutes of each day commuting on the school bus, while most of the other students boarded at the school. They came from all over the country and, in some cases, from other countries. Their families were very well-off, and it was not unusual to see many fancy, chauffeur-driven cars line the school drive, waiting to collect the girls at the end of term. Though I learned about wealth, I equally learned that I did not want to be the product of it. I was happy to return to my "normal" life, where my mother cooked dinner and I had chores around the house. At least there were only girls at school, so I did not have the pressure to look attractive to boys. I could focus on the task of getting through the system unscathed.

I met my first boyfriend at a mixed guide and scout camp. At thirteen, I was enjoying being a teenager, with all the changes that brought. While my father may still reprimand me, saying, "Young lady, let me never hear you using that tone of voice again," I was identifying as a woman. I felt my newfound sexuality and sensuality, realizing life's bigger game of love. Evident to the most casual observer is that all this attraction to the opposite sex was dangerous territory. Becoming a woman is never spoken about, never mind celebrated. I could only entertain boys in the lounge or garden, and sexuality was considered a dark art. There was no religious recrimination to guide my journey, but the family moral standard was a visible high ground with clear boundaries. There was a very long list of what young ladies should do and how they should dress and behave. How they should *not* behave was not even spoken about; it was simply unacceptable. Not to say I did everything I should, but I did know right from wrong and good from evil.

These were the years when I learned to split myself between what was considered socially acceptable and what was not. I developed an understanding that there was part of me I needed to hide, and even what I did show required continuous improvement to earn my place in the world.

How do we know what is authentically ours versus what domestication has created within us? Are we hardwired to evolve our consciousness until we die? Do we get a chance to review our practice, like getting a school report? Would there still be comments like, "Could try harder" and "Could do better if she talked less"? While I hope that just makes you smile, it is clear that we do not want the report to say, "She lived in fear, letting many opportunities to grow and learn pass her by!" To what lengths would you go to avoid that judgment?

Unfortunately, this narrative becomes part of our story and the one our inner judge takes on as something we can use to judge ourselves. We all tell ourselves lies and, far more dangerous, we honestly believe them. These roles of judge and victim live within us; we swing between them from moment to moment, making it impossible for us to win. The happiest moments come when we don't worry about the past or the future because we are fully engaged and enjoying ourselves.

"Living is easy with eyes closed, misunderstanding all you see ..."

~ John Lennon

"You should be ashamed of yourself." How often did you hear that as a child? How did it make you feel?

Are you letting your inner judge be the truth that guides you?

What comes from your head, and what comes from your heart?

How often do you let the real you come out to play?

Where do you still judge yourself and hold yourself back?

CHAPTER 4

THE BIG BANG

"We're all in the same boat – radiant and broken..."

~ Sy Safransky

1979

I get off the bus, ready to lug my heavy schoolbag the last block home, when I see my father's car parked and waiting for me. What a treat; this has never happened before. I am usually home long before he returns from work. As soon as I get in the car, I feel the tension; his face looks drawn. I immediately ask, "Is everything okay, Dad? You look worried?"

"It's fine," he says, his voice monotone, "Just your mother and I have something we need to talk to you about."

That is it, and I know not to pry further. We drive home in heavy silence, then he tells me to go to my room; he will be there shortly. I do so, collecting my brother from his room on the way.

My mother is nowhere to be seen. The two of us sit on my bed, both trying to guess what might be wrong.

I suggest, "Maybe Mum's had a car accident."

"No, she is home and her car is fine," my brother replies.

Maybe she's ill; we agree this is the most likely scenario. Minutes later, my father enters and has our full attention, as we expect bad news. Nothing, however, could have prepared us for the words that leave his mouth.

"I have fallen in love with another woman. Your mother and I are getting divorced. I will be moving out today but know it's nothing to do with you. I love you and you will be able to visit me as often as you like."

Silence follows as I attempt to get my brain to function. Maybe I did not hear correctly? I finally manage to blurt out, "Who is she?"

"Mrs. Grey," he replies and promptly leaves the room.

What on Earth just happened?!

I start to cry, and my brother hugs me. He, at ten, is being strong for me!

Mr. and Mrs. Grey were our family friends. They had emigrated from Zimbabwe, leaving without much, to the relative safety of South Africa. Mr. Grey came to work for my father and, later, Mrs. Grey also worked there as his secretary. My mother helped them move and get sorted when they first arrived. I could not comprehend this; as far as I knew, my parents were happily married. There was never an argument or a fight – at least not one we'd witnessed.

Needless to say, this news turned my life upside down.

As the saying goes, "What does not kill us makes us stronger"; however, some "life events," especially those experienced from an immature perspective, can shape our worldview, as this one did for me. I took my parents' marriage for granted. Mum, who had not worked since I was born, had dedicated her life to being a good wife and mother (at least from my point of view) and, like me, trusted this marriage to be a lifelong commitment. We were both rudely stripped of this belief, and she was devastated. There were no tears in front of us; she stayed strong, but her vulnerability scared me.

Shortly after the divorce, an envelope addressed to me arrived in the post. I immediately recognized Nana Gee's handwriting – as most people recognized the writing of those they received cards and letters from in the days before email. Even today, I remember my grandmother's home address by heart. I tore open the envelope, eager to read her words to me.

My Dearest Joanne,

Thank you for your lovely letter you sent me, yet I have taken so long to reply. I am now finding it terribly hard to sit down and write at all, yet I must try and get in touch with you, so I can send you my love and God's blessings. Try as hard as me, dear, to carry the heavy cross that has been put on us. I pray each hour of the day for you all. Do help each other. Do so wish I had someone to talk to. The sun still shines outside here, but not anymore in my heart. Good to know it is sunshine time in your country. In thoughts with you each hour my dearest granddaughter, we have each other to bless. Try hard, dear. With my best love for you—xxxx.

She died six months later. I had such a special relationship with my grandmother. Even though we lived in different countries, we did get to see each other during holidays and communicated regularly through letters. It is hard to compare this with the ease with which we now communicate worldwide, in real-time and at no cost, thanks to the internet. I still recall so many small details, like her bringing me tea in bed when we stayed at her house; this would never have been allowed at home.

Most importantly, I knew how much she loved me and all her grandchildren. Her passing did not feel real – perhaps because we were face-to-face so rarely – and I often thought to write her a letter before remembering, with a start, that she wouldn't be there to receive it. For the first time, I thought about the possibility of what happens to us after death, as I wanted so desperately to communicate with her. I felt if there was ever anyone I would be able to connect with afterlife, it would be Nana Gee. Alas, this was not my experience, but it did spark my interest, and I started to explore and read stories about reincarnation.

Auntie Pam was also part of the deep, loving family net that held me at this difficult time. "How suddenly you have had to grow up!" she wrote, "It is so much nicer to be a little girl, isn't it? I have heard how much you have been able to help your mother during the last few weeks. It is very strange when you realize that grown-ups make far worse mistakes than children and that they need you almost more than you need them. I know that your father has gone away but I am sure he still loves you very much and will go on loving you…"

My family nucleus shattered; I brought my walls of protection closer, to surround only myself. I decided it was vital not to rely on any man if I did not wish to suffer my mother's fate, and from that point forward I dedicated myself to the goal of independence.

My father remarried immediately after the divorce. The following years were turbulent as my brother and I tried to find a place between our parents. Our first big challenge was addressing our new stepmother. She was still "Mrs. Grey" to us, but to call her that would be weird as she now shared our surname and of course, neither of us would call her Mum, as we already had one! She permitted us to use her first name, but that felt so awkward we simply avoided addressing her directly whenever possible. We took separate turns trying to live with them, and both had miserable endings. I was slightly envious of my stepmother's children, who were much younger and better able to adjust, referring to their "old daddy" and "new daddy." On the other hand, my brother and I felt like we did not belong anywhere; we were just uncomfortable reminders of a past best forgotten. Things only got worse when Dad and Mrs. Grey had a son together and we children were designated "his," "hers," and "theirs." My little half-brother was certainly the lucky one, living with happily married parents and blissfully ignorant of all that had come before.

I learned to take nothing for granted and knew that trust could be easily misplaced. But life went on, and I continued to navigate these insecurities as I explored myself in relationships with others and the world.

Looking back, I can see how easy it was to see myself as a victim in this chapter of my life. I felt that none of the mess around the divorce was my fault and my family seemed to agree with me. Little did I know then, I was completely responsible for how I felt and reacted. We are born with the instinct to keep ourselves safe, but following this instinct often comes at the expense of experiencing life fully. I suggest watching Oprah Winfrey interviewing Elizabeth Gilbert (*Eat, Pray, Love*) about the pain she felt after losing the woman she loved. Gilbert stated so clearly, with such impact, that she had to get to the point of welcoming everything, even the pain. Life is a package filled with all sorts of experiences; to live it fully, you can't be selective. In England, there is a brand of sweets called Liquorice Allsorts. They were created in 1899 when an employee supposedly tripped over and spilled a tray of samples, mixing the various candies. As he picked them up, the color of the assortment inspired him. Life experiences are also a mixed bag and, like every assorted packet of sweets or biscuits, we have our favorites and those we'd rather not sample again. Still, we must taste it all lest we miss out. Hopefully, we can get to the point where we are glad everything happened, as it is all learning.

> *"Have enough courage to trust love one more time and always one more time."*
>
> ~ Maya Angelou

Is it better to have loved and lost than never to have loved at all?

Would you rather not trust a person to avoid being deceived?

Given a choice, would you rather live a married life in anxiety and distrust, or live in contentment and trust, even if it ends in betrayal? Not an easy question to answer, but it may be valid if we instinctively protect ourselves from hurt or heartbreak.

Do you experience your life fully, without trying to pick and choose just the "good" parts?

CHAPTER 5

GENDER DIFFERENCE (EARLY WORKING YEARS)

"Don't ask what the world needs. Ask what makes you come alive, and go for it. Because what the world needs is people who have come alive."

~ Howard Thurman

1982

I am applying for a position as a computer programmer, and I really need the job. When I'm called into the office, the manager says, "I am sorry, but there has been a mistake. I am only interviewing men for the position; they should not have sent you." I ask why, and he says, "There will be night shifts and it is not safe for women to travel alone at night." I suggest that if that condition of employment (night shifts) was apparent in the advertisement, then only those prepared to take this risk would apply, and it should not be limited to men. I hope this gives him something to consider, but it won't influence my application.

At this moment, I feel very aware of being a woman and how this might limit my options.

Girls and boys from my society and generation were given different career options at school. There was an overlap where girls could consider science, law, or medicine, but I did not presume it was always easy to study and work on a level playing field in these professions. A colleague once told me how strange she found it that in England, all the secretaries were women, whereas, in India there was a much higher percentage of male secretaries. I suddenly realized that I too had hidden stereotypical ideas of gender and profession.

At the time, I was serving as Chief Information Officer and head of Information Technology. One day, I was speaking with the director of the company's human resources department. She asked if I'd gone to an all-girls school, and when I answered in the affirmative she smiled and told me about a study she'd read. It found that women who went to girls' schools had a significantly increased chance of reaching higher management positions than those who did not. The researchers postulated that this was because the students did not experience the gender divide regarding subject choice and options. Without the competition and comparison to boys, they simply did their best. I didn't know if this was true, but it did give me lots to think about.

I remember sitting at a boardroom table surrounded by men while waiting for the meeting to start; they laughed as they told jokes that were rude and certainly not meant for women. I was almost offended when I realized the paradox: then in my thirties, I had spent years trying to prove myself as equal and capable in this male-oriented profession, and clearly I had succeeded. They treated me like one of the boys, no longer seeing me as the woman I was! I realized how difficult it was to be feminine and accepted as equal.

Reflecting on these years, I am exceptionally grateful that I found something I was good at and built a career that took care of my family. In *The Big Leap,* Gay Hendricks differentiates between our "zone of excellence" and our "zone of genius." The former is seductive and traps us from finding the latter. I guess I would never have had the courage to think of what I did as "excellence," but I knew I could do my job without constant struggle. I mostly felt pressure from my workload and not having enough hours in the day to finish the work. I had taken aptitude tests and, again, was grateful to have found something I could do. I never even thought about the possibility of looking further. I did not expect to do something I loved. My understanding was that you worked to live – "fun" had nothing to do with it.

I can't write about gender discrimination without touching on racial segregation, though admittedly I wish I could put my head in the sand, ostrich style, and avoid it altogether. The truth is nauseating and incredibly uncomfortable to discuss.

I was born in South Africa, knowing I did not have dark skin but not seeing myself as "white" either. In fact, my skin color seemed impossible to name, and while I was not proud of it I was certainly grateful for the opportunities it afforded me – I would never experience the injustice of discrimination. Given the choice of how I would look in another life, I would love to have beautiful caramel skin. White skin is not attractive (well, at least mine is not), but almost transparent, with every vein visible. We ladies all know the slimming effect of wearing a pair of black trousers.

How can I claim to be a non-racist when born in apartheid-era South Africa? "I do not know" is the honest answer, and though I had no choice in the matter I have to take some responsibility. Having British parents who treated everyone with equal kindness and respect, I never felt it as a child. How is my white culture influencing my life? What makes me "whiter" in my perception and awareness than my first cousins born and bred in England? What did I inherit from this strange culture and what confusion have I passed on to my own children? Once, when we flew to England and landed at Heathrow Airport, my daughter, with her South African passport, had to go through a different border control line than I did with my British one. She had to complete an entry form and check a box on a list for "Race / Ethnicity." I waited a long time for her and had to ask permission to go back through security to find what kept her. She could not complete the form, not knowing what box to tick, as she was not on the list of options! She was not European and equally not Black African. There was no box for 'White African," thus she was stuck. What a world we live in where a child has to classify herself, and how dull the world would be if everyone were like me. Nothing is more exciting and inspiring than to meet people from other cultures worldwide.

Don't confuse sameness and equality. At the end of our apartheid years, we were so traumatized and sensitized to be non-discriminatory we could not describe the apparent differences. When describing a missing person, they would refrain from mentioning he was Black and say only that he had short, dark curly hair! It is like describing a vase of flowers and explaining their shape and fragrance without saying they were pink. Once, on holiday with friends from abroad in a South African game reserve, we had fun joking with them. We explained the way you can differentiate between male and female zebras. The males are black with white stripes, and the females are white with black stripes. It took quite some time of careful observation before they realized the joke. I feel the same with ethnicity, black on white, white on black, and anything between. There are, of course, apparent differences between us, but they have little to do with our skin!

We are all quite different in how we look, even if we are all made of the same "God stuff," and nobody is any better than anyone else. We are equal while also being vastly different.

Whatever we consider a human right should be required as a base law in all countries across the globe… not such a simple concept as we look at the Taliban taking control of Afghanistan. We can see clearly that women's rights are quite different under Islamic law. We can see a difference without choosing right from wrong, and we would need to agree on the basics worldwide! Anyway, it's an interesting concept to think of a world law where we could all be global citizens. Maybe this is where we will have to go when forced to share some of the significant issues that face us now. We cannot fix the global climate change crisis any more than we can combat global pandemics at a national level. We must unite, recognizing we all share the same planet, or we stand no chance.

I was listening to a discussion about women, their value, and their place in the economic world; it seemed women were always asking questions to validate their equality. The answers made it clear that our physical differences only matter or are of any importance in bedrooms and bathrooms; in all other places, it should only be a matter of competence. We should all be concerned with our masculinity and femininity; keeping these vital energies in balance and flow is critical for our health. People so often confuse masculine and feminine energy with gender.

After not having a vote and/or opportunities in many professions for much of our history, the challenge of striving for pay equal to men's seems minor in comparison. It is important to me that competence or capability should not be pre-judged by employers based on gender. When there is heavy manual labor and muscle power needed in a job, we may consider it a man's work. Yes, men, on average, are bigger and stronger than women, however, some women are more able than men and should get equal opportunities. Moreover, the workforce looks very different today – whereas we once relied on "manpower," then "horsepower" and heavy machinery, we now have computers and robotics to assist us. Technological development is one driver of the change, and new professions now exist that I never imagined when I left school. We need very different skill sets in this new world. You may even choose to be a nanotechnologist. These do not all need big muscle; they do, however, need specific competence. So now, more than ever before, if women concentrate on education, training, and helping our children move beyond the limitations from the past, exciting times lay ahead.

I invite you to watch *Hidden Figures*, a film about three female African American mathematicians who worked for NASA in 1961. Amazingly, they were called "computers" because of their brilliant, sharp minds. Another film, *On the Basis of Sex*, is the true story of Ruth Bader Ginsburg, the second woman to serve as a United States Supreme Court Justice. The film is set in 1956, when Ginsburg, who graduated top of her class at Harvard Law School, could not get work in a law firm because she was a woman. These movies are stark reminders of how restrictive things were and how far we have come.

> "No one is born hating another person because of the color of his skin, or his background, or his religion. People must learn to hate, and if they can learn to hate, they can be taught to love, for love comes more naturally to the human heart than its opposite."
>
> ~ Nelson Mandela

Have you experienced inequality and been discriminated against?

Were you given a wide range of career choices, or limited by gender norms?

Do you spend your life doing what you are good at, or what you love doing?

Have you lost touch with your natural genius trying to be someone else?

Twenty years from now, will you be disappointed by the things you never tried to do?

CHAPTER 6

'TIL DEATH DO US PART

"Expectation is premeditated disappointment."

~ Sogyal Rinpoche

1984

It is a perfect day. The sun is shining, and everything is picture-perfect. I don't feel like the bride I am, but a witness to this event. I look around to see all the beautifully decorated tables around the garden swimming pool and the guests, all of whom seem to be having a good time. I find it strange there is only one table for our friends; the other guests are friends of my father and stepmother. Some, I don't even know. Though I'm very grateful that my father afforded me this white wedding, I'm also aware that it's not really for me, but for appearances. They can have a party while seeming to be doing a wonderful thing for their daughter. I feel comfortable in my dress but had no part in choosing it; it was second-hand, kindly sold by my stepmother's friend. I don't care about this; I take a deep breath and smile, knowing this is the start of my new life with a family I will create, independent of this old mess. Choosing between my divorced parents will no longer be my only option.

The divorce had divided family, possessions, and even friends! The master of ceremonies is an old family friend who, after the divorce, "sided" with my father. My deep thoughts are interrupted by his tapping a champagne glass to silence the chatter of the guests. Once all eyes are on him, he clears his throat and says, "Thank you all for coming on this very special occasion. I am only sorry that Joanne's mother did not see it fit to attend her own daughter's wedding."

Blood drains from my face; my heart is pounding so hard I'm sure others can hear it. I am so angry. Was that necessary?! Many guests don't know the messy backstory and can't possibly understand the complexities. I understand exactly why my mother didn't attend, and I know it would have been awful if she had. The rest of the speeches continue, but I am not even listening. I am no longer fully present; I just want to get this day over with and escape. I need to cry and let my feelings out without spoiling the day for everyone else.

My commitment to Independence didn't end with my marriage. Though I wanted a happy family, earning my own money (thus ensuring I was never vulnerable if I found myself alone) was vital. I never wanted to be in a position where my back was against the wall. I left school and immediately found a job, as I could never have imagined asking for help to fund further education. At this point, I wanted nothing from anyone. On the other hand, I can now look back on my twenty-year-old self, marrying a good, kind man I had been friends with for years, and see that it was an escape. My half-brother had his first birthday the same month as our wedding – a most telling "coincidence."

I also deluded myself into thinking I could be married and remain completely independent. "No man is an island" is not just some cliché but actually backed by science. We need only look at the interdependence that exists in nature to see that it is all about balance. Of course, back then I was not ready to contemplate any of this, as I was still living in a state of struggle and fear.

The foundation of independence is sovereignty; we want to rule ourselves. This is not just a personal quest – our history books are filled with struggles at a national level or by groups within nations. Nobody likes to be told by someone else what they can and can't do. If there must be rules, then we can at least demand we are part of their making. Self-rule may be the same as self-realization. We desire freedom to come into a place of choice. Some of us have forgotten how to stand in our power. We have a collective wounding so deep we often forfeit sovereignty in order to be loved, accepted, or even liked. To take control of our lives, we must also be able to say no and maintain our boundaries, protecting them from outside invasion. When you stand in a place of sovereignty, you stand in a strength that needs no pushback and no force.

To be feminine is to connect with the cat within. No one ever "owns" cats; they are independent, loving, graceful, and capable of looking after themselves, but they still know how to find love and get pampered.

How much have you given up to please others?

Do you stand in your full power without needing to be aggressive?

Do you feel part of an interconnected, interdependent "worldwide web"?

CHAPTER 7

PREGNANCY AND CHILDBIRTH

*"There are only two kinds of people, those
who have known love and those who haven't."*

~ Paul Newman

1987

I wake up in a pool of sweat; my pajamas are soaking wet and I'm shaking uncontrollably. What is going on? I can't even focus enough to see the bedside clock. I have never felt like this before. I don't know what this is, but it is not good at all, and my breasts feel like they're on fire. I wake up my husband and, at three a.m., we decide to call the doctor. Thankfully, the poor man answers. (These were the days when doctors still made house calls and would answer their own phones in case of an emergency.) I explain my situation, and he tells me I have mastitis, or "milk fever," and need to go to the hospital to get antibiotics. I must also stop breastfeeding my baby for the next two weeks!

How had I managed to get into the situation? I had foolishly taken a male doctor's breastfeeding advice as gospel! He told me to express the remainder of my milk after each feeding to avoid the milk glands getting infected by the "old milk." How ridiculous is that? I did this religiously, often while sleep-deprived and exhausted in the middle of the night. Of course, I now know I was telling my body that I had a starving baby who needed more milk! Even all these years later, I can't believe my naivety – or that my children survived it. Now, I would recommend accepting guidance on mothering skills only from a woman who has successfully cared for children.

I had my first child when I was twenty-three; I was free of my childhood drama and making my own family life. I honestly have very few regrets in life, as I recognize everything was essential in bringing me to this point, but oh, how I wish I had been wiser and able to make better decisions to support my firstborn. I still revered the superior knowledge of doctors and trusted their guidance without question. I could write a book about everything I learned as a new mother. I felt it unfair to have been given this precious gift without a user's manual to refer to!

I only followed the script of my cultural path. Even though I wanted children, I cannot say I consciously conceived them. I did what all girls did: grew up, got a job, left home, and found a man to marry. Then, it was not *if* we would have children, but *when*. There was always the question of whether I could conceive, but this was not in my control. Ours was only to try, and I never seriously contemplated not having children – a generational and cultural thing, I know.

I conceived my first child while I was still using birth control – evidence, in my mind, of high fertility. I was, therefore, shocked when I had two miscarriages trying for my second child. Emotional trauma goes hand in hand with miscarriage, and I decided an only child was not such a bad option. There would have been four or five years between them at this time. Then I thought of my mother and her brother, separated by eleven years. Though they had not grown up together, they had a relationship and were there for each other when their parents were gone. I knew Mum valued having a brother. Convinced of the benefit of having a sibling, I tried again and finally carried my second child to full term.

My husband and I watched *Woman in Pieces*, a film about a woman whose baby daughter became distressed during a home birth, did not get enough oxygen, and died. Needless to say, it was disturbing and sobering to be reminded of how fragile and risky the process of bringing new life into the world is.

It is so easy to get complacent in our modern world. I never considered that the baby or I were at risk, yet both girls I delivered had complications. The first was a difficult forceps delivery, where I needed internal stitching to repair the damage; sitting was a big challenge in the first weeks after the birth. My second child had the umbilical cord around her neck, which the doctor needed to cut before she was fully delivered. Both needed experienced doctors, and I was relieved to be in a hospital. That said, there are more comfortable places to give birth, and it is much better to have the freedom to move around in privacy. Tribal women never experience childbirth alone; they always have many experienced women elders to support and help them. I was surrounded by men or at least male doctors; the only women were nurses there to assist him, not me. That was thirty-six years ago, and much has changed since. When my older child gave birth to her daughter, I was with her right to the end, when she had an emergency c-section. She too was lucky to be in the hospital; she was in labor for three days! My younger daughter took time to decide if she wanted to have children, but at thirty-one she could already feel the internal clock ticking. It seems a little unfair that we have to decide early or take the possible risks associated with pregnancy in older women. Women over thirty-five are considered to have a "geriatric" pregnancy! Still, many more women are now waiting to complete their education and establish their careers before making this big decision. Of course, deciding is not all it takes; we can try to procreate but quickly realize how much is not in our control.

A Place to Call Home was a television series where a pregnant woman is kicked in the stomach by a Nazi prison guard. The baby dies as a result, but she still has to go through labor and deliver it stillborn. Much later, she adopts an unwanted baby as her own. I felt that labor scene so profoundly, like it was me. How much pain and drama do we hold collectively around sexual mores and trying to control our reproduction? Women have been trying to understand how NOT to get pregnant for centuries; in the early 1900s, birth control was relatively primitive or not accepted. Women often had more children than they wanted or could afford. My husband's grandmother had twelve children in twenty-six years and recalled how she cried every time she learned she was pregnant!

We do not "make life" – we can plant a seed and create optimal conditions for it, but whether it grows is another matter entirely out of our hands. Life chooses life. I loved the idea of a soul looking for a body, choosing parents and players for its life experience. Dr. Wayne Dyer told a funny story where his daughter was unhappy with him. He pointed out that she had chosen him, so she only had herself to blame. Not missing a beat, she retorted that she must have been in a big hurry and would be more careful next time. I had no idea about the truth of this concept, but it was at least fun to imagine!

Parents may do what they think is best for their child but often need clarification on the relationship. Kahlil Gibran, author of *The Prophet*, said it best when talking about children: "They come through you but not from you, and though they are with you, yet they belong not to you." So often, we wrap all our hopes, fears, failures, and missed opportunities around our children, ensuring they do not make any of the same mistakes we did, while taking their success or failure as our own. I used my childhood experience as a template, or a basis, at least, for my parenting. While you frequently think you could do better than your parents, you still use them as role models, and off you go. I never thought about a child's full potential being a miracle to keep active and open; I had no such grand ideas.

Being a parent tops the list of the most challenging jobs we can have. It also provides lifelong learning; the key is to realize it is the child teaching you, not vice versa. Think about being "fully formed." Teaching is all about informing others, assuming you know anything in the first place. Then you intend to push your conclusions onto another's mind. Sharing information is like casting others into stone. The world needs us to become more open-hearted and more open-minded. Let us open to getting rid of all our hard-earned conclusions. Every conclusion is like a period at the end of a sentence and marks the end of an inquiry. Once you believe something, you do not need to look any further. As our minds get stuffed with fixed ideas and beliefs, it is quite a physical thing too; we become less flexible and lose our agility. Of course, aging plays its part, but just think about how active children are.

How much easier could you move as a child compared to now?

Think back to your childhood. When did you stop playing? When did you stop imagining? When did you stop running for fun?

We are domesticated from an early age. When were you told when to stop playing, how to behave, and to take responsibility?

CHAPTER 8

HAPPY FAMILIES

"Appreciation and gratitude are a must if you choose to become the architect of increased happiness and your own fulfillment."

~ Doc Childre, founder of HeartMath

1988

I look up from what I'm doing in the kitchen and see, to my horror, my daughter launching her chicken in the air. She is on the step outside the back door, and before I can wipe my hands to get out there she has caught the poor bird again and is about to repeat the exercise! She stops mid-action as she hears me shouting, "What on earth are you doing to that chicken?"

She innocently looks at me and answers, "I'm teaching it to fly."

We had stayed for a year in a small flat and saved every penny to self-build a house with cash as we earned it. Luckily, my father-in-law had gifted us a property to build on, making this a possibility. The effort to build this house alone cannot be left as a single sentence in this story, as it represented many years and occupied every part of our young married life. I drew the plans and got the design passed; my husband did the build with help from casual laborers to mix mortar and carry bricks. We got started without experience and only a bricklaying course to guide us. Moreover, as we had no evidence of our competence we could not get a loan from the bank, which is why we had to build as we had the money. Only when we got to roof height were we able to get an inspection of the building and secure a mortgage to complete the roof.

It was winter, and the long, dry grass had burned down, leaving just black stubble on the ground. One day, while out to see how the building was progressing, I walked away from the house, looking through my camera viewfinder, making sure I could get the entire house into the picture frame. The next minute I looked beside me; there was a Rinkhals snake, hood spread at waist height, looking straight at me! Like a spitting cobra, this snake is quite venomous, and this particular one must have been about a meter and a half (or four feet) long. When faced with a snake you should freeze; however, while the brain may well know this, in that instant, the body reacts before the brain can even engage. I moved so fast I may have broken the sound barrier! I screamed so loudly that I was not sure who got the biggest fright, me or the snake. The point is that I'd luckily left my fourteen-month-old daughter close to the house with her father while I took photographs. I do not know what I would have done had she been with me. I, of course, like to think my motherly instincts would have kicked in, but I was grateful not to be tested.

We decided to move in as soon as we had windows and doors installed. We could then save our rent money and live in the house we were still completing. The property still had no mains water or electrical services, which made this a huge decision. There was a borehole that pumped underground water to a big tank that was close to the house. Here we filled containers to take inside for drinking and general use. We also had a kind neighbor who let us run a long extension cable to get our electricity temporarily; that was enough to run the fridge and freezer. We had yet to put in the ceilings or even paint the walls; it was a shell of a home, and living there was like long-term camping. We had a portable chemical toilet like the ones used in camper vans, which could have been better. Still, we managed, thanks in part to regular visits to our parents' homes to enjoy a hot shower. Getting the mains water and sewerage connected was a high priority. Getting the electricity connected took a year! Each day I would arrive at work looking like every other employee, and smiling at the thought that they had no idea where I had come from and how much effort it took to get to that point in my day. We spent every night after work and every weekend working on the house. We played "musical rooms," moving from one to the other as we completed them. For example, the kitchen started in the dining room, and we ate there too.

Slowly but surely, we made progress and had a home to be proud of. Funny how the tough times can also be the happiest ones. The challenge keeps you focused on something more significant than your little day-to-day tasks. We worked hard and raised our children as best we could, but we never worried about putting food on the table or paying rent we could not afford.

During this period, we got a rabbit for each of the children to dissuade them from having dogs or cats as pets. We reasoned rabbits would take little upkeep and happily roam free in the garden. This idea worked quite well, as the children loved them dearly. Unfortunately, this story ended unhappily when they found the rabbits dead one morning; we assumed a dog or big bird had found a good meal. This was my daughters' first lesson in death and the impermanence of life, and it caused much heartbreak. My younger daughter asked her father if he could fix her broken rabbit!

We then tried chickens and the children named them Claude, Candy Floss, Frederick, and Feathers. It was Feathers that my youngest daughter was teaching to fly; the same bird, that on another occasion, I found her holding while rubbing her foot on its feathers to soothe a bee sting! Feathers did not seem to be bothered by this new use of her soft bottom feathers, presumably preferring this to the flying lessons.

Looking back, even when life seemed to be going well, there was always a feeling or question in the back of my mind about whether it was too good to last.

Maybe this realization comes with age and not just having children, but we get to a point where we are made wise by the responsibility of our future. The illusion of being in control of your life might drive you to work harder and ensure the happiness of those closest to you. Whatever the case, failure no longer feels like an option. While there is something or someone else dependent on us, we strive not to disappoint anyone.

> *"The grand essentials to happiness in this life are something to do, something to love and something to hope for."*
>
> ~ Joseph Addison

Have you ever felt uncertain, even in quiet and relatively stable times?

When have you felt most at peace?

Who are the most important people in your life? Do you feel responsible for their happiness?

CHAPTER 9

BACK TO WORK & LIFE LESSONS

"Let your river run, sister. It is not what you think. There is still life waiting for the miracle of grace and the touch of springtime long buried but never vanquished."

~ ALisa Starkweather

1989

My daughter is just three years old. As my mother is getting dressed, my daughter notices she has something stuck on her skin; this is her hormone replacement therapy patch. Curious, my daughter asks, "What's that?"

My mother answers without a moment's hesitation, "Why that is my label, everyone has one." Looking genuinely concerned, she asks, "Don't you have one? Where is yours?"

The child says, "No," but does look under her dress and takes another good look to be sure.

My mother says, "Oh dear, I guess your mother removed your label, she must just remember when you were born and how you need to be washed."

The story about having a personal label is hilarious because I realize how labels make me crazy. I have sensitive skin, and they always scratch me. The very first thing I do when I buy new clothes is cut out all the labels!

When my first child was born, I took maternity leave. At home with my beautiful baby, I reached the end of three months and had difficulty weaning her from my breast milk. I could not see a way to express enough to feed her while I was at work and, more importantly, I could not get her to drink from the bottle! What a stressful time that was. My mother challenged my need to go back to work. Remember, she had always been a stay-at-home mother for her children. She was not pushing me in any direction, only insisting that I admit I had a choice and wanted to return to work. That was simply not true! I was so angry; I told her we had bills to pay, and my salary was not just "nice to have." She was still unconvinced, and I even offered to show her the proof of our monthly expenses. She did believe we were spending the money, but she pushed me to admit that I was working for our lifestyle.

We chose the home we lived in; we decided on the cars we drove. Our lifestyle was our choice, and we were working for that. Now, I do not want you to think I was living in luxury. We were still desperately trying to finish our first home while living there. I drove a second-hand car and never spent money on high-dollar clothes. Still, all that aside, the point was clear: I worked for more than our basic needs. I could have been a stay-at-home mother had I chosen a different life. Instead, I decided to return to work and leave someone else to look after my baby because I wanted a particular standard of living. All these years later, it is still hard for me to write that. Living with yourself as a victim is much easier than accepting accountability. I appreciate that teaching now, but I certainly did not at the time.

As a child, if I stubbed my toe on a step I would yelp and exclaim, "Stupid step!"

I never got sympathy for such injuries; I got reprimanded for placing blame on an inanimate object. "Don't blame the step. It did nothing. It is your stupidity." I knew that, of course, it was just a reaction, but I'd hurt myself; could we not have just focused on my pain? A silly example, but the lesson was clear: there is always an opportunity to take responsibility for everything in my life.

Responsibility is different from taking the blame. My cat got lost or ran away, and I was upset. Was that my fault? No, it was not, but I was responsible. I like breaking down this word as it helps me get this concept better, response-able. I am "able to respond"; I get to choose the meaning I make in any situation, and I get to choose my experience. If I do not take responsibility, I deny myself the possibility to choose my response, and automatically, I become a victim because I have no control. My cat may have left because he was free and not kept in a cage. I loved my cat, but he was only mine when he chose to stay. Something terrible may have happened, but I had a choice of how to feel about it; I loved and missed him. Once I realized I was responsible for my life and chose all that surrounded me, what then? Well, I recognized myself as a gatherer of things. I accumulated things that may have made me happy or even excited me for a while, but just as their newness could not last, neither could the emotions I felt when I first got them.

My mother has always had a beautiful relationship with her grandchildren, so when I went back to work I assumed, with my mother not working herself, that she might offer to look after them at least one day a week. No chance. "You had them," she said, "You look after them." She explained that a parent's job was to bring up their children, discipline them, and teach them manners. She would have a relationship with them, but not that of a part-time parent, where she had responsibility for their discipline.

I cannot say this sounded very reasonable at the time, but now I fully understand. She would spend time with them and, so long as she was not on holiday or otherwise engaged, would aim to take them one afternoon a week. Interesting that she decided to take them separately. Given the five-year age gap between them, she recognized they would benefit from doing different things with her and value the time away from each other (wise woman). It was precisely that; they loved it and looked forward to their days with Nanna. It was not necessarily the same day of the week that she took them, and being inconsistent was utterly useless as far as help with childcare was concerned. The point was clear: it was not about me, but the relationship she chose to foster with her grandchildren.

No matter how beautiful and shiny they look when they are new, things in life still look old or tired in time. When there is something our heart desires, we focus on acquiring it. We may continue appreciating things, especially if they provide comfort or protection. I mean the roof over your head or clothes that keep you warm. There is, however, a significant difference between things that meet our basic needs and everything else. The power and value of the wheel transformed our lives, but a great majority of us seem to have created much the same thing within ourselves; that's why so many identify with feeling like they are living inside a hamster wheel. The same cycle repeats day after day. Your choice may be to slow down or speed up; there appears to be a choice of what you look like and what comforts you might enjoy while you run. The more you earn, the better the running shoes you can afford. You may be able to run faster than another, in more comfort, but we are all still treading the same path, and round and round we go. Awareness of where you are and where you are or are not going is the first significant step in breaking the cycle. Then we are faced with the choice. Can we get off? It is better to slow down before you decide to change, or you could get hurt.

When you move slowly and have time to think and look around, you might start seeing other options. Moving from certainty, even when it's monotonous and exhausting, to the unknown takes great courage. It is vital to be bold enough to follow the compass of your joy to find and contact whatever attracts you the most.

Things can feel unjust at the time, but looking back, you can see their value and reason. Think about this possibility the next time you feel things are not fair. Often looking at a larger perspective and seeing beyond yourself helps.

> *"Nobody can go back and start a new beginning, but anyone can start today and make a new ending."*
>
> ~ Maria Robinson

When was the last time you felt unfairly treated or like a victim of circumstance?

What does it take to recognize patterns and make the choice to change?

Do you need faith in the larger field of life to feel safe enough to move into the unknown?

Do you trust that someone has your back and will always be there to support you?

CHAPTER 10

END DATE

"With the new day comes new strength and new thoughts."

~ Eleanor Roosevelt

1995

I don't know what hit me, but it's not good. I don't feel pain, yet I can see my right hand is bent backward on my arm, looking like it does not belong to me. Using my left hand, I reach for my face and feel the glass. I look at my fingers, now covered in blood; I have a brace on my neck; unsure if this is a dream, I try to focus. A nurse approaches, asking if she can call someone for me. I struggle to think. Telephone number recall is challenging, but I ask her to phone my husband. Off she goes, but returns later with the news that not only was my husband not at work, he was out of the country! I had forgotten this. I then give her my mother's number, and off she goes again. I lay there, trying to take it all in. I remember a round light, like a full moon above me, and a man saying, "Don't panic, you were in a car accident, it took some time to get you out, but you are safe now, in an ambulance and we are taking you to the hospital." I asked if my children were with me, and he said I was alone in the vehicle. Thank God. I can recall no more of the journey or arriving at the hospital.

Here I am in the chaos of accident and emergency, left to put the fragments of my shattered mind back together, clearly not made easier by the morphine that courses through my veins. I am reliving the crucial moments in my life and feeling the emotion of each one, not just mine, but how others were feeling too. I can feel the web of life and how deeply each ripple affects others. My daughters are three and eight years old; they must still be enjoying themselves at school. I will need my mother to collect them and take them home until my husband returns. The nurse's voice interrupts my deep contemplation, asking if the number I gave her for my mother is correct. She has tried for hours, and the line is constantly engaged. Good, at least this means she's at home; I reassure the nurse this is normal and ask her to keep trying.

I was fortunate to survive the crash, but sadly, the driver who hit me did not. My car was a write-off, and my body took a long time to heal. Thank heavens, I do not remember what happened at all. Luckily, there had been an off-duty police officer in the car behind me, so he could stand witness that I was not at fault. With a broken wrist and pelvis and my face peppered with glass from the shattered windscreen, I had weeks on my back to contemplate what I most valued in life.

During my stay in the hospital, I got to know all the staff and regularly saw new people brought into my ward. One day, the nurses settled a new patient into the bed next to mine, and she was in an awful state. She almost looked like one of those cartoon sketches of the person in hospital with bandages from head to toe, one leg raised in support, and limbs in plaster casts. When she could talk, I asked her what had happened.

She worked as an office cleaner, and at the end of the day must have been in the ladies' or unnoticed and was locked inside. Already it seems unbelievable that those closing the building would not check first before leaving. Panicking because she had children to get home to, she shouted and screamed for at least an hour, but nobody heard. Finally, she decided her only option was to jump out the window! She was on the second story of the building and did not know how much she was risking. She realized it was high and thought she might hurt herself, but she underestimated what the impact would do.

Wait, I could not understand. Why had she not used the phone? There must have been phones in the offices. Imagine my shock when she explained that she knew neither how to read nor use the phone! I do not think ever, before that day, had I stopped to think about illiteracy as a disability. Wow, I could suddenly, at that moment, comprehend how it must feel not to be able to pick up a phone and call for help. Still, how could you jump from that height without understanding the danger to your body when you hit the ground? Was this also education, something I learned at school? I do not think so; I am sure I got this somewhere during play. Sobering, to say the least, that I could live side by side with people and have so little comprehension of the lives they lead.

My husband and I had taken Joice, the lady we employed to take care of the children while we were working, on holiday with us to the seaside. She had never before seen the sea, and on the first morning, in our holiday home right on the beach, I found her standing at the window, mesmerized by the waves. She said she could not sleep at all. I worried the bed might have been uncomfortable, but she explained she did not want to stop watching the water, to discover when they would stop playing! I loved this, and again realized how much understanding I took for granted. Joice also taught me cultural differences when we discussed sending invitations to a wedding. This practice in her culture is inconceivable, even rude. If you are inviting some, then, by definition, you are not inviting others! She asked me with a very straight face how we decided where to cut the family. Of course, I protested with all the standard logistical arguments to defend our practice. How do you cater and provide for an unknown number of guests? Of course, you simply give all you can afford, and everything will be okay on the day. Most critical is that every person who wants to be there, can be. I assume this wonderful tradition must come from a time when villages were small, and everyone knew each other, and of course, invitations would be unnecessary. She did finally admit that today the expense of a family wedding could be crippling and, very often, the family would go into debt trying to provide an appropriate feast for vast numbers of people, some of whom they might not even know!

After spending many weeks in bed healing, I painfully learned to walk again, and this was no small feat. At this point, I promised never to wake up in the morning without being grateful just to be able-bodied. A few months later, I was back to normal, with day-to-day stress, worrying about work issues or problems I could not solve. How quickly we forget to be grateful for good health.

Few people have a clean bill of health, and life leaves its scars. My injuries, other than those I sustained in the car accident, include torn ligaments from skiing accidents, broken bones from a cycling accident, stitches from falling in the bath as a toddler, and two incidents rescuing cats (I should have known better after the first time). The critical learning is that when we or any other creature is feeling threatened, all reactions come from a root level, survival instinct. The famous fight-or-flight response happens automatically, triggered by a perceived threat. There is no possibility of engaging the logical mind or differentiating between friend and foe in this place of acute stress. Where my instinct was to help, I would have been better off learning the lesson, first stepping back and waiting to see if the cat wanted my help.

While I knew I would die one day, I had only woken up to the reality that it could be any day as I faced this challenge. Life is precious, and I realized I needed to choose, with great care, how I spent it. Never mind a Happy New Year; I should celebrate every "happy new day." Every morning that I got to open my eyes I should appreciate the precious gift it was.

Though I can't know your innermost desires, I can guarantee your dreams and aspirations are the best clues to lead you to discover your mission in life. Take the time to find out what brings you joy. You can blossom precisely where you are without waiting to be where you want to be. A present is a name for a gift, and it accurately describes being in the now moment.

Contemplate what it means to have fun, not just enjoyment or being happy. Maybe there is an element of something unknown when we have fun. When swimming in the sea, not knowing how big the next wave will be, or playing a simple game, waiting to see how the dice will fall or where the ball in play will go next. Even blowing bubbles and not knowing where the wind will take them and how long they will last before they pop can be fun. Why does it take significant events to wake us up? Like being warm and cozy in bed on a winter morning, it is not always an exciting idea to get up and get going; sometimes, we need to be encouraged. Most of us don't even realize we are sleepwalking. Become aware by becoming more conscious of life, discover the ability to lose your identification with your mind, and instead come to your senses.

> *"Life is pleasant. Death is peaceful.*
> *It's the transition that's troublesome."*
>
> ~ Isaac Asimov

What makes you feel excited about being alive?

Have you had a time when your health or circumstance stopped you in your tracks?

Do you have a "bucket list" of things you want to do before you die?

Are you living a life worth remembering?

CHAPTER 11

HISTORY REPEATS ITSELF

"There is nothing like an intimate relationship to let us know that we're not as developed as we thought."

~ Robert Augustus Masters

1998

The dinner was good; my husband and his friends shared lots of laughter, but I felt no part of it. We leave the restaurant and stroll through the mall together. All the shops have long closed, and my husband walks laughing and joking with his friends and is flirting with his young secretary. I lag back, watching from a distance, and no one even notices I am no longer with them! At this moment, I realize, in a flash, that my marriage is over. I feel sick to my stomach, but it is suddenly painfully obvious. I had tried so hard but failed to make him happy. Right now, with friends, he is the life and soul of the party. Yet back home, he will again be miserable and assure me that it is not my fault and it has nothing to do with the children. I feel so hopeless, but I am not helpless. Even if I am not the problem, this is an unhappy relationship I can't seem to mend.

When we get home and are alone, I share my feelings and tell him I want a divorce. He denies having an affair with this pretty young woman; perhaps, but he has lived with her since the day he left us and moved out, less than a month after this awful night.

I experienced the painful feeling of failure; the fact I tried hard counted for nothing. I was not naive; I never expected a perfect marriage, but I did, however, believe very strongly that I would never get divorced and cause my children the same pain I had suffered. Now, as I ate humble pie, I realized marriage is more complex. Our divorce went through the day before our thirteenth wedding anniversary. I honestly felt relief to no longer be responsible for trying to make someone else happy. The only promise I made to myself was to ensure I always kept a civilized, non-antagonistic relationship with my ex-husband, for the sake of our children. He rapidly found a cash buyer for our family home, and we had to move out with only two weeks' notice!

I was terrified. What was available to rent with what I could afford looked dreadful. My elder daughter helped by collecting boxes from the local shop on her way home from school so we started packing all our belongings. At only eleven years old, she needed to grow up quickly and was a great support. I remember her repeatedly saying to me, "Don't panic, don't panic, don't panic," always causing us to stop and laugh; if you do not laugh, you will cry. Our good friend, whose parents had a flat on top of their double garage, came to our rescue by offering it to us at an affordable rent, and we moved in immediately. We benefited from their home security and had views of their beautiful garden and swimming pool without any ownership, maintenance, or stress. Once again, I had evidence that I was magically supported when I needed it the most.

I was brought up, like many others, to believe good marriages are all about give and take.

I remember a line in the Robin Williams movie, *License to Wed*, because its truth struck me deeply. "Marriage is not about being happy. It is about having someone to blame." Wow, that is huge, and it occurred to me that it may also apply to the work we do. What if I got something more from my work than income? It is great to have to work to earn a living. Everyone understands why we are working, and we get to be justifiably tired at the end of the day. The other unobvious and possibly hidden benefit is that I don't need to try and do anything else of greater importance in the world. I can hide behind my work, saying, "I would do something else if I could, but I can't because I need the income." I have created a perfect cover and an excuse not to fail or take risks.

Some twenty years later, I was deeply upset by *Poldark*, a historical drama set between 1781 and 1801 in Cornwall, England. The wife, playing the lead, does something to help a friend that, unbeknownst to her, badly impacts her husband's business. He won't forgive her, no matter how hard she tries, leaving her trapped in a loveless marriage. I wanted so badly for her to walk out, leaving him to realize his stupidity and her value in his life. Getting divorced was not possible for women then. She would have been at enormous risk alone, forced into hard labor, and that, only if she managed to escape being taken back into her father's ownership, and he was awful! Just imagine the lack of freedom and choice! When we're unhappy with what we have, we need only look back at our recent history to be grateful for how far we've come.

I had to swallow a bitter pill of humility as I learned the hard way not to judge my parents' failure at keeping their family together. I recognized very clearly, for the first time, a pattern repeating itself. Did my need to be independent prevent me from relaxing into the sanctity of marriage?

I have no regrets because this marriage gave me two beautiful children, but I realized I was responsible for this divorce. I jumped into marriage to escape my mess, out of need, where I was unhappy with myself. I did love this man, but there was an arrogance in feeling *I* could help *him*! I was sad and alone but had at least been given another chance. Freedom of choice is beyond value.

I found myself, during this challenging time, in a place of deep inquiry about the purpose of my life. When I learned of "Awakening to the Dance of Life," a self-empowerment workshop held by a hypnotherapist, energy therapist, and counselor, I signed up. This would be my introduction to the power of energy healing and, through the people I met, the ancient art of Reiki. This 2,500-year-old practice, rooted in Japan, aims to improve the body's energy flow. It helped me relax, finding relief from my stress, and the fact that I could feel the heat of the healing hands without physical touch was enough to inspire my curiosity. I decided to learn more and got my Reiki Master Teacher attunement, enabling me to practice healing and teach others. However, I did not pursue this then, as my full-time career and single-parent responsibilities took precedence. It was the first time I recognized my body being more than the physical; there are extraphysical "layers" that are integral and vital to our lives. Philosopher Rudolf Steiner referred to the etheric body as early as 1910. While I still identified my body as who I was, at least the boundaries of what I thought of as me were expanding.

Family disintegration is a challenging subject to discuss. We often refer to a dysfunctional family, but I am unsure what defines this. We can imagine the perfect family, but complicated ones are more typical than we might like to believe. Family units are organic, living things; they change, grow, and divide constantly. I wonder if we can use divorce rates as an indicator or measure of family stability. There must have been broken relationships when divorce was socially unacceptable, as was pregnancy out of wedlock. We have this deep desire to keep things steady and constant. We want our family units to be something on which we can depend. While families do, no doubt, provide a frame and structure, expecting them to remain constant is naive. Some family shifts are like waves; grown children leave home, and marriages, births, and deaths are regular events in all families. However, some changes are more like earthquakes, which cause permanent damage to those directly impacted.

Perhaps the biggest strength we have is in partnership. I love balance in all things, maybe because I am born under the Libran scales, and the masculine and feminine are no exception. This is not to be confused with male and female as both genders can aspire to balance their masculine and feminine energies. Still, there is some gift in the union of two individuals. Why do we desire to find our "one true love"? Love seems to be an unstoppable force, driving us to momentary craziness and questionable judgment. One fundamental instinct is to procreate, but we have our own needs too. Hormones have hijacked our intelligence; we try to choose a partner to fulfill us, making us feel whole and complete, with a complicated bundle of expectations, often at a subconscious level.

Contemplate the need for a committed relationship. What if we found a better reason to join our lives, not to complete each other, but to grow as we journey together, not headed toward each other, trying to get ever closer, only to face an inevitable crash?

We signup for marriage or partnership with an obvious expectation of what the other should bring to the party. We must each work tirelessly to live up to the other's invisible expectations and keep that happy, "in-love" feeling. Are we set up to fail on this mystical mission, doomed to disappoint each other sooner or later? We can switch from love to bitter resentment at any point. We then have a choice to either run away or grin and bear it, based on our promise to say together, "'til death do us part," not happy but committed. We also use this word when sent to asylums; it makes me think. How can I make any promise for tomorrow if it is right now, only in my imagination? Don't stay with me because of some old commitment; instead, make a daily choice because there is nowhere else you would rather be. The idea of marriage or any committed relationship is to multiply your joy, not share your misery.

> *"Life has taught us that love does not consist in gazing at each other, but in looking outward together in the same direction."*
>
> ~ Antoine de Saint-Exupery

Have you grown cynical and jaded through a love you thought would bring everlasting happiness?

Have you had the experience of not getting what you wanted and then realizing it was what you needed?

CHAPTER 12

LOCK THE DOORS

"Love or fear ... the decision defines you."

~ Oprah Winfrey

1999

The automatic garage door clunks to a close. I leap from the car and rush into the house through the back door. Without switching on a light, I run into the front room to peep out the curtains, where I can see the road and driveway. My heart is pounding. Did I imagine the menace in that man's eyes in a split second as our cars passed each other? Did he innocently turn around, not following me at all? Am I stupid and neurotic? Oh my God, there he is; the black BMW slowly drives past. This road is a cul-de-sac; he's not just passing; he's looking for me! Thank heavens, I trusted my instinct and immediately turned off my headlights, hoping he would not see me turn into my road. Luckily, I did not have a front gate to stop and open, or I might not have made it. I shake and shudder to think I may have just narrowly escaped being raped or even worse.

People often ask where I am from; when I say South Africa, there is a moment's silence, and they ask, "Where are you *really* from; where were you born?" It is still surprising to some that I can be African and have white skin!

South Africa is a truly magnificent country, known as the cradle of humanity, and even those not born there often report feeling a deep sense of belonging. Many refer to this land of hope and glory as the "Rainbow Nation" – a term coined by Archbishop Desmond Tutu in 1994, the year apartheid officially ended. I love the rainbow as I get all colors mixed in one without choosing a favorite. Nelson Mandela proclaimed that each South African is intimately attached to the soul of this beautiful country, just as the Jacaranda trees of Pretoria and the Mimosa trees of the bushveld; a rainbow nation at peace with itself and the world. But I was not at peace with myself living there.

I was born to a nonracist family, guilty by default because of my European race. As a child living in a distorted, segregated, apartheid world, I was oblivious to it. As an adult in this new democratic nation with Nelson Mandela as president, I felt like every black person still looked at me as a thief, having taken something rightfully theirs. I could not be with any native South African without feeling exposed and wishing I could explain how I felt. I want to say, "It wasn't me," but it was. I was living in their country, or so it felt to me. Those victimized by years of unjust oppression fostered resentment and hatred. I did not belong where I was born and was part of the problem; at least, this was my experience.

As I look back on our life in South Africa, there is only one way to explain the developments and changes in the country, which is to unravel it backward slowly. It is like unpicking something knitted with a pattern or picture. As you pull the wool, unpicking every stitch, you see where the pattern came from. I grew up in a very safe environment with only minor crimes, yet when I was twenty we lived behind electric fences and burglar bars. I can actually track the changes as they happened. As a young child, I remember we didn't need to lock the car when we popped into the local shop; the house was only locked up when we went out.

One day, when I was about ten years old, I answered a knock at the front door. A man stood there and said he wanted to speak to my mother; she was in the back garden, and my dad was in the garage. I could not shut the door in his face, which would be rude, and I could not ask him to come through the house with me, so I asked him to wait while I called my mother. When she came to the door, he was gone, and so was her handbag and many other things within easy reach in the house, and she was very angry with me for being so careless. So, we learned to keep the front door locked if we were in the back garden and not simply trust anyone who came to the door. Then there were burglar bars. First, it was only necessary to put bars on the small opening windows in the house to stop the glass from being broken and simply open the window latch from inside, allowing easy access. They did not need to look ugly; the ones in my childhood home were wrought iron with soft curling patterns, and the house we built when I got married had square bars that mirrored the windowpanes. Then there was another issue: if you opened the front door, you might not be safe. We solved this problem by installing security gates, so you could open your door and speak to someone but not need to open the metal gate until you were sure it was safe. Things still got stolen, but that was inevitable living in a country with so many people who had less than you with a massive gap between the "haves and have-nots."

When car theft increased, we developed intelligent controls, a trip switch, that if a thief hotwired a car, it would only drive for five minutes and cut out. That made things worse as to steal a car successfully; they needed the vehicle while it still had the keys in the ignition, not parked and secured. They would then resort to holding the driver at gunpoint when stopped, force them out of the car, and take it! My ex-husband survived this trauma, having a gun at his head and his vehicle stolen in his driveway. These were called hijackings, and there were plenty of them. An article in the Guardian in 2006 stated that 16000 cars were stolen this way in 1998, which is still a significant issue today, even during lockdown! We learned to change our driving habits as we were most at risk at night and we learned to slowly approach a red traffic light to avoid having to stop. Wait till the light turns green before approaching the intersection. When you get home never pull up to your driveway gate so that someone could pull in behind, trapping you. Stop parallel to the house, in the road still facing forward, get electric gates fully open, and ensure there is no one behind you before you pull in. Always drive with your doors locked, and keep your driver's window open a fraction so somebody cannot simply smash the glass.

I always felt most vulnerable if I got home late and the children were asleep in the car; I would have to unlock the house and carry them in one at a time. I remember a couple's story about having their car stolen from their home. The next day, the vehicle was returned with a note from the thief, explaining their plight and giving them two cinema tickets as an apology. In this instance, you can feel sympathy for the person in such a desperate situation that he needed to steal a car! Feeling fortunate to have their vehicle back, they saw the film. They came home to find their home empty; even the fitted carpets were gone! There were many housebreaking cases at night where people were at home sleeping. Theft while you are out may be one thing; being robbed if you are at home is quite another. My friend and work colleague had her house broken into when she was at home with her young children; they were unharmed but gagged and held at gunpoint while the intruders took what they wanted from the house! Others I know were less fortunate, where a woman was raped by all the intruders in front of her husband before they left. This kind of trauma can destroy a family and cause fear, hate, and resentment. At this point, we took the security to another level; my mother put a gate in the passage to block access to the bedrooms. One night, she woke up hearing someone in the house. I remember my mother being so angry on this particular occasion when she discovered the following morning that the intruder had taken time to eat cheese and biscuits in the kitchen. At this point, we have electric fences and an alarm system, but still, it seems insufficient. When we built our home, I did not want an ugly metal security gate in the house, not only for the aesthetics, but I did not want to be visible on the other side. If I heard someone in the house at night, I needed to get the children from their bedrooms into mine without being seen. We put a solid wooden door in the passage to block access to all the bedrooms, which we locked every night when we went to bed!

Have you ever justified a crime? "Well, you can't blame them for breaking into the house we have so much, and they don't maybe they were hungry." So clearly etched in my mind came such an awful incident just around the corner from where we lived. Armed men robbed our local shop of cash – unfortunately, not an unusual event. What was unusual was that, as they left, one shot a pregnant lady through the stomach. I feel sick again as I write this, and I cannot find anything to explain this brutal act. This young woman could not possibly be a threat to them. Worse even than shooting to kill, they aimed at an unborn child. I decided that only an intense level of hatred, beyond my comprehension, could trigger such an action.

It seems crazy as I write this now, but it just crept up on us, it happened slowly one day you are safe and the next thing you know you are living behind bars with electric fences, guards on call and are still not safe. I love South Africa and never felt like I was living in fear. As I write this, I even feel like a traitor saying such dreadful things about a country I love. I had hoped that as things settled in a post-apartheid era the country would prosper and there would be less crime as the wealth became more evenly distributed. Now look at the crime numbers they still show year-on-year increase with the South African police service reporting 18,162 cases between April 2019 to March 2020, that makes me incredibly sad. Such a beautiful country now firmly under the leadership of the African National Congress and there is still this level of crime. I am proud of the country, like a parent of a child, but it is hard to show off the good when there is still this evidence of social disease. Who would want to visit reading this? It is a beautiful country and perfectly safe to visit if you take some basic precautions.

My father told me, "Don't wait for an opportunity; look for one. I had my working life and can live in this country with a good pension, but you still have your career ahead of you; why not earn a decent currency? I would be far happier knowing my granddaughters will be safe; I would hate for them to become a statistic. Keep your counsel and do not go telling everyone your plans, expecting support. You may well get lots of criticism, but it is your decision. I don't see a good future here; with so much uncertainty, it is simply not worth the risk."

I valued his advice. Is the difference between an immigrant and a refugee simply timing?

Continually being in this disharmony is a "dis-ease" and feels like it will make me ill if I don't move away from it. As I planned to leave my country of birth, I realized I might never belong anywhere, but I needed to be free of this feeling of guilt. I got married to separate myself from my family of birth; then, I got divorced and separated myself from the family I created, and now I plan to be separated from my country. I felt like a particle spinning ever further away from the nucleus. How far can it go? Would I ever find rest?

Cultures are curious things, and when we put them together, they don't immediately mix. One culture seems to be the oppressor that seeks to dominate the other. The oppressed feel a bitter, growing resentment that festers, leaving both cultures living discordantly. When we pushed ourselves into another culture without invitation, we were naturally in the minority (we politely referred to this as colonization). To keep safe and hold on to what we had found, we rapidly had to invent systems to separate "us" from "them." How could we control them and keep ourselves protected? Looking at these cultures, I see that this function, or dysfunction, evolved over generations.

Race was invented in the mid-1600s by the elite class in early America designed to divide and subjugate the working class, to segregate and keep control. The significance of race seems more relevant in countries that outsiders conquered, the nature of the native people alienated and suppressed. I think many countries have the same history of separation and segregation, but in some countries where everyone belonged, the distinction was not about racial color; here, it became about class or caste.

We mainly associate caste with India. In her book, *Caste: The Origins of Our Discontents,* Isabel Wilkerson speaks about the original bipolar system of segregation in the USA. Things got complicated by others moving into the system and needing to be classified, deciding how they could be positioned relative to others. Is this why we refer to being an outcast, literally those who have been rejected or ostracized by their society? Maybe it is rooted in being cast out! Do we have this caste system in all cultures? The other day I was watching a program about a well-known, renowned matchmaker in India. A lady from Guiana was looking for a partner while living in America. Her ancestors were all Indian, but the matchmaker had extra challenges finding her an Indian man to date, as her caste was unclear!

All this is a symptom of fear, triggered by what we can't identify with or control. If we see a dead bird next to the road, we may notice it; if we see a dead dog, it can upset us more; but if we see a person lying dead, that stops us in our tracks as it is a significant event! I used this extreme example to demonstrate how we are affected differently by our identity.

> *"Man gets lost, settles abroad,*
> *goes so far out he cannot get back again."*
>
> ~Meister Eckhart (c. 1260–1328)

Do you have the courage to be free?

What is the hidden price of feeling safe and being in command of your life?

CHAPTER 13

DIY

"The Ocean is smart – the waves recede to gather energy for the next one."

~ Carol Stakes

2005

Finally I get to take a deep breath. I have survived my divorce. I have successfully emigrated from South Africa to England. My ex-husband has immigrated to Australia, as this was something we had considered before we got divorced and had gone through the huge effort to get "leave to remain" visas in Australia for our family. My daughters are both doing well at school and I am managing to make ends meet. My fear of failure and finding our family living on the streets is under control. I know I can manage my job well; even if it still holds some pressure and stress, it is what can easily be described as normal. As I now look at my life and see, I have my wonderful family and my work, but not much else.

I had dedicated most waking hours to the big project I was managing at work, and I spent my weekends washing, cleaning the house, shopping, and then getting my daughters back to school on Sunday afternoons. I often needed to rush directly to the airport to catch a flight to wherever I needed to work the following week. Still, I was at least starting to think of life outside of work, looking at where I might be able to do activities, meet people, and make friends. I joined the local ramblers, enjoying some fantastic guided walks in the magnificent Surrey hills where we lived. It was a gift to walk so many miles in the beautiful countryside without even figuring out a route or worrying about getting lost. I also joined a cycling group, which became an excellent opportunity to explore a slightly wider area within a forty-mile radius of my home. I met a lovely divorced man with children a similar age to mine who lived with their mother, so he could cycle with me and enjoy the weekend fun.

Although we did not live together, we maintained a steady relationship. For many practical reasons, I found it so much better to be with a partner. As a divorced woman, I was just a little socially unacceptable. Nobody said as much, but I knew friends did not invite me to dinner parties as it made their entertaining awkward with an odd number of guests. He and I had an unspoken understanding that neither of us was looking for marriage. I still found myself, after several years together, wondering if it could ever be something more permanent. Being in a long-term relationship where commitment was not on the agenda, left a gap that I knew I wanted to fill.

In the meantime, my daughters were becoming more unhappy as they had to leave home and return to their boarding school every Sunday night. I was also exhausted with this continual business travel, so I started looking for a change in my work, to allow me to spend enough time at home where the girls could attend a local school.

I found this excellent opportunity to take an assignment managing the IT department for the same company in their Belgium office.

While this did mean that we would have to move again, and we did not speak the local language, it still felt safe because the company guaranteed our return at the end of my assignment. I managed to sell this move to my daughters. I took time to explain that, like Switzerland, Belgium was also home to delicious chocolate, and we would all be able to live at home together, with them attending the local British School of Brussels. While this may seem simple on paper, the devil was in the details. My relationship had to end as he had to continue working in England, and this was also an emotional stress for me. As we had made no commitment to each other, I felt it was better to cut ties and stand as a single mother again, focusing on my children while settling in a new country.

Imagine my surprise when he called, some months after our move to tell me some "good news." He had managed to get a work transfer to his company's Brussels office so that he could move in with us!!! After all the trauma of our split, he returned, just like that, and without even discussing it with me. Looking back, I might have said, "Thanks, but no thanks." Instead, I found myself simply happy to have support, although he flew home frequently to see his children and still had his own home in England, we made it work.

We joined a local cycle group that I am sure would not have worked as well if I had been a single woman. I even referred to him as my partner, as having a "boyfriend" at my age seemed silly! I thought all I needed to do was love someone enough, and I would get love in return, but this is not how it works. I got exhausted over-giving and settled for a partnership where true love eluded me. I guess we both knew it was a relationship of convenience, each preferring that rather than being single, but after years of on-again and off-again, it finally ended for good. In my search for meaning and health, I decided it was better to be alone and enjoy solitude rather than settle for being with the wrong person. I wrote in my journal, "Single again, on the greatest journey of my life, to find myself!"

I found time for self-reflection, searching for something more than simply working to earn a living. I felt myself running on the proverbial hamster wheel, exhausted as I tried to keep up with the demands of life that left me feeling unfulfilled and uncomfortable. In an attempt to get out and meet people outside of work and get fit, I found a Pilates studio in Brussels. I could not believe how quickly I got into shape, but more importantly, I felt a core strength and more balance in every aspect of my life. I learned to breathe consciously, breathing in life and breathing out mental pressures and aggravations.

Most importantly, I saw women of all ages in great shape and could imagine a future where I could also teach Pilates in a future chapter of my life. With the seed of possibility planted, I started my Pilates teacher training, which was a real highlight of my Belgium work assignment.

This journey, I found, included challenges stemming from the move, including differences between school exam boards at the British School of Brussels and the school my children had left back in England. For my eldest daughter, now in the final years of her school education, some subjects could not simply be switched mid-year as the coursework and curriculum are very different. When it came time to apply for university entrance, I also discovered, they would be international students, because we were no longer UK residents. As such, there was a substantial financial increase in the university fees.

This "simple" decision I made to leave England would have huge repercussions. My elder daughter decided to use her Australian resident visa, still valid as she was not yet an adult, and got accepted into Brisbane University. I was distraught that she was leaving, but I held on to two little things that helped me find the courage to let her go and say goodbye. Firstly, I hoped she would get to know her father better. He might also step up and fund her university education since he had yet to manage to help support the children up to that point. Secondly, she had a boyfriend who was entitled, lazy, and, in my opinion, drank too much. I was happy her decision would end the relationship without me needing to get involved. At the time, she was sure she would remain in Australia only for university, after which she would come home.

Of course, this is not how life works; she moved, studied, met a man, fell in love, and married. Now they have two beautiful children, so with an all-Australian family, there is little chance she would ever leave.

The law of unintended consequences played out in my life as this four-year work assignment in Belgium splintered our already dispersed family and spread us to yet another continent.

Do we pretend that love is not what we are searching for? The harsh truth is we can't find love outside if we have not first learned to love ourselves. We have to give up something to make space for a loving relationship. Give up not feeling good enough and not believing you are beautiful and capable just as you are. Stop over-giving and trying hard to prove yourself.

As we go through life, we can't pretend we did not get damaged on the journey. It's interesting to think about the word "recover." If we recover something, we find it and get it back. Recovery has nothing to do with fixing, so our recovery from things that have injured us is just a process of restoring what we already have back into balance. Let's be proud of the stories our scars can tell, just making sure they are not open wounds to be easily infected again. Imagine yourself like a tree that gets damaged by a strong wind. The tree needs a support stake while it heals and strengthens again. If not removed in time, this same support can cause other problems when the ties that hold it prevent further growth.

The art is knowing what no longer serves you and having the courage to follow your guidance. The adage "Better the devil you know than the devil you don't know" limits our ability to explore and find new exciting adventures.

> *"Don't settle for love of this or that, he or she; that is all so, so small. Stubbornly hold out for love itself – beyond everything."*
>
> ~ Bruce Allen

Have you looked for love in vain?

Have you found yourself stuck in a situation, not knowing how to move on?

CHAPTER 14

SELF-WORTH

*"The mind is its own place and, in itself,
can make a Heaven of Hell, a Hell of Heaven."*

~ John Milton, 17th century poet

2009

The smell of fresh ground coffee and warm pastries fills the morning air as I enjoy the company of my colleagues. Just twelve of us, selected globally, received the IT Excellence Award and a special Harvard training as our reward. As we assemble around the boardroom table, I can see the Rhine and the distant snow-capped mountains. I'm not sure it gets any better than this. The facilitator then asks us to introduce ourselves and share something we are most proud of that is not work-related. I am the last in the round, and each person's story seems more incredible than the previous one. We have a fighter jet pilot, a classical pianist, a cardiac heart surgeon, and an environmental toxicologist!

I am no longer listening as panic sets in. What on earth can I possibly say about myself? My mouth is dry, and my heart is pounding. It is finally my turn, and after hesitantly describing my courage to move to England as a single mother with two young children, I move on to my parents' successes: my mother's effort to save trees and help women needing wood for open fires with her non-profit solar cooker business, and my father's successful plastic injection molding business, started from nothing. The rest of the training is a blur. I am happy with myself but don't feel like I belong here. Some strange luck got me this far. I was only exposed to a small group today. I must keep this job, as I might not be this lucky again. I take a deep breath, close my eyes, and am reminded not to get complacent and feel comfortable in this position. I may be on the executive twelfth floor, but this is a glass house, and I could come crashing down anytime!

Later that night, my head was still spinning, and I wondered why this was such a challenging day. Of course, I was very proud of my children. I had two beautiful daughters who were strong, independent, and talented. They had never gone hungry, always had a good roof over their heads, and I had provided them with the best possible education. If I was proud of them and they were fantastic, that must be at least fifty percent me! Looking at my parents, the same was true; I hold fifty percent of each of them, right? So why could I be proud of everyone around me yet find it so difficult to be proud of myself? I somehow managed to earn my place at the table. Maybe it was simply fear of failure and hard work alone, but I would not have been there unless I added value to the company. At that crucial moment, under pressure, I had managed to swallow my shame and honestly voice what I could. After the session, I was amazed at how many people thanked and congratulated me. I was proud that I had managed to surround myself with people who inspire and interest me and make a difference in the world. I fell asleep feeling deeply grateful for my life and everything in it.

Life lessons don't just take a sweet linear upward path toward self-love. We do not get to conquer the fear of being judged or not being good enough; one time and it is done. We store feelings of inadequacy in every cell of our bodies, and as soon as the mind thinks it is all sorted, it pops up again to surprise us. We can recognize that we are not even able to master ourselves! While working hard at everything around us to create a good life, we cannot even control our minds. When we are vulnerable and connect authentically with others, our seemingly separate lives become more meaningful. If we trust the greatness of others, then we have to see some reflection in ourselves.

> *"Love is based on our capacity to trust in a reality beyond fear, to trust a timeless truth bigger than all our difficulties."*
>
> ~ Jack Kornfield

Have you ever made one small mistake or experienced an upset that keeps replaying again and again in your mind, even to the point of keeping you from a good night's sleep?

Do you recognize your self-worth and see your true divine nature?

CHAPTER 15

CONTROL

"Everything that slows us down and forces us patience, everything that sets us back into the slow cycles of nature, is a help."

~ May Sarton, famous poet,
and author 1930 - 1959

2010

I am young yet feel very old; I look fit and normal but need a disability badge! I find myself sitting on the floor at the airport, waiting for my bags. People stare. I don't care; I have no choice. I have no energy and struggle to walk for more than a few minutes without getting out of breath, and I struggle to work full-time with lots of travel.

Once again, I am desperate for help and try explaining my total exhaustion to the doctor: "I did what you suggested and took a holiday for a week, and I'm worse, not better."

The doctor replies, "You need more than a vacation; you must take a year's sabbatical to rest completely. We might even consider treatment for depression. Women, at a certain age, can often no longer cope with a high-stress career. Women cannot take the same pressure as men. I saw so many of them drop out of med school. They may be smart enough, but they do not have the stamina and all it takes to stay the course. I had a lovely doctor that worked for me. She managed through university, but when it came to the daily pressures of clinical practice, she finally had to step out and take care of other family demands." I am at a loss for words. Seeing my blank expression, he clarifies, "You know, divorced, or single woman headed towards forty, without support." Lucky for him, my condition is exhaustion, so it prevents me from leaping over the desk to throttle him!

My mind is spinning; I can't even think about a year not working! I am a single mother and need to support my children! "Thank you doctor; I have lots to think about," I say, leaving the consulting room, feeling helpless and hopeless.

I was not stressed, other than not knowing what ailed me. I was not depressed either. Depression is when you can get out of bed but don't want to. Exhaustion, you want to get out of bed and can't.

The holiday I just had was with my mother, who was visiting from South Africa. I had not enough energy to walk down the beach with her and the kids! My desperation was evident to her when I sobbed in pure despair after the children went to bed one night.

I found another local doctor, a lady who did a lot of blood tests and diagnosed chronic fatigue syndrome and fibromyalgia. The oxygen level in my blood was so low she was surprised I could even leave the house! I shed tears of pure relief, finally knowing what was wrong with me. On the other hand, the cause was unknown, and she could offer no treatment beyond diet and a potent vitamin regimen.

My mother flew back to South Africa and popped in to see a friend on her way home from the airport. She explained my poor health and discovered her friend's son had the same issue as me! She recommended a book, *A Disease Called Fatigue* by Cécile Jadin, that led him to a precise diagnosis.

Cécile Jadin, a surgeon born in Burundi, had practices in South Africa and Belgium. She also seemed to have medicine in her blood, as her father was a researcher who specialized in tropical diseases at the Pasteur Institute. Jadin's connections to the countries I had lived and worked in seemed to indicate I was on the right track, so I immediately scheduled an appointment at her Brussels office. Blood tests confirmed I had contracted Rickettsia, similar to Lyme disease, most likely originating from a tick bite. It is difficult to fight this nasty condition, as pathogens penetrate the cells and are not freely available to kill in the bloodstream. This disease was starving my organs of oxygen and could actually kill me if I did not get it under control. Extreme antibiotic therapy was prescribed, to the horror of my local GP, who thought the treatment would kill me even if the disease didn't. Getting to this point, with such an incredible string of synchronicities, left my mother believing in miracles too!

I know doctors do the absolute best they can. I cannot even imagine how difficult it must be to operate in a vast bureaucratic system that dictates how many minutes they can spend with each patient! My youngest daughter made me laugh; sitting in the doctor's office one day, she looked at the grand certificate framed on the wall behind him and said, "What is a hypocritic oath?"

I grew up trusting doctors to be highly educated people who knew everything beyond question. A brilliant physician, the Chief Scientific Officer where I worked, laughed at the idea of getting a single diagnosis for any significant health issue. He pointed out you may get at least three opinions and quotations even when needing your car repaired. I better understand why they are medical practitioners, as they are still practicing, which is valid for all of us. We are all practitioners of life!

Even with Cecile Jadin's treatment, I would spend several years recovering and getting my life back on track. Rickettsia forced me to slow down, which, though tough at the time, I now see as a gift in disguise. We are always in a rush, trying to work, care for family, and keep healthy. It is indeed good to take time to stop and smell the roses. We all know this saying, but how many of us do? When your body takes charge and slows down, everything becomes enhanced. When it takes a great effort to do something, there is an excellent incentive to question the necessity for any action before moving.

When I could finally let go of the idea of control and accept what happens as neither good nor bad, just what is, I would be free. Then I could focus on the detail and pay attention to the beauty of everything around me. Smell the yeasty fresh bread baking, see the hydrangea with its new buds, showing signs of life after winter, and the bulbs popping out of the cold ground… and smile. Watch the birds doing spectacular fly-bys and singing their hearts out every morning… and smile. I took a deep breath and looked again at my current situation, knowing I could navigate it. As they say, "It's all good in the end, and if it is not good, it is not the end." This challenge would also pass and be a blessing, even if I could not see it that day.

Finally, this illness had brought me to rest. I had felt like a particle spinning ever outward, not dead-still, just reaching the perfect point to pause before starting another cycle. I felt the rise and fall like a long slow deep breath, held on fullness, or the waves of the ocean that crash onto the beach, that seem to momentarily pause before being drawn back to the sea. This quiet still space, allowed me to find the next level of self-awareness before moving forward on my life journey.

The path to healing is itself a great teacher. To heal means to make whole as we wake up to our true nature. The Hebrew word *tikkun,* which means fixing for the sake of repairing the world, reminds us that this journey is greater than ourselves.

Being healthy is not just about the body; it alone does not give us purpose but enables us the energy and vitality to fulfil our purpose. We desire healing to prevent the body from getting in the way of what we choose to do. While it is not always possible, as soon as we start working with our bodies, there is a powerful symbiotic relationship. You might know you are not your body but know for sure your body belongs to you and is the only one you will have in this lifetime. Often what we resist persists. Integrative medicine focuses on the whole body, recognizing that it is not only what disease the patient has but what patient has the disease! Beth McDougall, M.D., suffered from Lyme disease, and her path back to wellness gave her the opportunity to explore the most fundamental factors affecting our health. She published a fantastic book in 2021, *Your Pristine Blueprint* that I wished I had been able to read during my recovery. Brilliant minds are constantly pioneering work that transcends our current understanding. There are incredible examples of people with extreme disabilities that still make a difference in the world. Think about Stephen Hawking, Helen Keller, and Beethoven; the list could go on. Tenacity and the fortitude to never give up are essential.

Even without accident or disease, the body won't last forever; like your car, it has limited "mileage." The choice is how we use every mile efficiently and maintain the vehicle to optimize the available time without problems or breakdowns. We operate like solar-powered vehicles, so we best understand how we generate and consume energy. Imagine having a gauge so that at the end of the day you could measure the number of breaths – positive, negative, and neutral. When you got ready to go to bed at night, you could be super proud if you had spent most of the day in the green high-efficiency band. You would be carbon-neutral if you could stay present and at peace without worry and stress. Now, if you could get to happiness, joy, love, and laughter, this could boost your energy. At this point, you would have generated surplus power and be able to give back to the grid. You would then be an energy supplier. Isn't that a sweet thought?

We cannot choose what happens in our lives, but we can choose how we respond. "What doesn't kill us makes us stronger" sounds logical but is stressful, nonetheless. Stress seems to be born from feeling out of control, and while this could be a simple opportunity to trust it takes practice to see it as thus and, in fact, can feel like an impossible challenge.

Another adage – "Everything is going to plan, just not our plan" – also rings true. We just gradually see that the unplanned twists and turns bring us to the precise place we are today.

If you pay attention to all the details, you cannot help but see the tenacity of life. It shows up where you see a plant managing to grow halfway up a solid rock wall or weeds that find a way to grow between the roadside paving. Watch the birds, the bees, the plants, and the wildlife that surrounds us. They are always busy, living life to the fullest. We can see how much there is to live for when we pay close attention to these little things around us. As we see them, the essentials do not always go to plan; loved ones get ill, accidents happen, work gets tough, lovers come and go, and life unfolds in magnificent complexity. While we may well participate in the game of life, we are not the master controller. What might be a personal disaster may be great news from another perspective we can't see.

> *"Security is mostly a superstition. It does not exist in nature, nor do the children of men as a whole experience it. Avoiding danger is no safer in the long run than outright exposure. Life is either a daring adventure, or nothing."*
>
> ~ Helen Keller

Would you choose to do something different if your body did not restrict you?

When have you felt out of control and stressed by the experience?

Have you ever looked back on a roadblock in your life and recognized the gift it presented?

CHAPTER 16

SELF-LOVE

"You're off to great places! Today is your day! Your mountain is waiting, so ... get on your way!"

~ Dr. Seuss

2011

I take a deep breath. These days, we "click" countless times a day – some frivolous, others requiring genuine courage – this was the latter.
I look at the words, "Your reservation is confirmed," and think - *Did I just do that?* I pour myself a generous glass of wine. I never drink alone, but this is an exception. My heart is beating fast; I'm very excited. Jack Johnson is singing "Staple It Together" in the background, keeping me company as I get my head around my big new adventure. No depressing, stereotypical celebrations with family and parents for me this new year – I am off to California! I choose to be with like-minded people who inspire and interest me. The "human potential" retreat will be held at the Asilomar Hotel and Conference Grounds in lovely Monterey from the 28th of December to the 1st of January 2012. Some of the authors I most admire will be there, including Ken Wilber, who is headlining the event. Wilber's book, *Integral Life Practice,* is a framework for understanding

ourselves and the world in which we live. I'm especially excited that Barbara Marx Hubbard will be in attendance. Not only had I read many of her books, I had spent nine months completing her online course, "Agents of Conscious Evolution." I can't believe I am going to be able to talk to her in person!

Immediately, my guilty conscience kicked in. I had just spent money on an international flight, not to South Africa to see my mother or Australia to see my eldest daughter and granddaughter. I started reciting Ho'oponopono – "I'm sorry, please forgive me, thank you, I love you" – repeatedly. Ho'oponopono is a beautiful practice of forgiveness from traditional Hawaiian culture that can be practiced alone or with others. The intention is to "make things right" or cause things to return to balance for yourself and the other person.

Eighteen months of intense antibiotic treatment was not easy, and it took time to recognize my fear which was so strong, understanding that I could not remove this destructive organism living within me. I contemplated the acronym for FEAR – False Expectations from an Artificial Reality – but my reality felt all too real. During the enforced slowdown when I was ill, I had taken time to read many books, and Marci Shimoff's *Happy for No Reason* was like a breath of fresh air that made perfect sense to me. I wrote in my journal, "I have decided to be the real me! I grow stronger each day through a powerful healing regime of Pilates and meditation, feeding my body alive, healthy foods that create vibrancy and longevity. I can't become myself by myself." I was happy and at peace; though not yet healthy, I controlled this disease enough to feel my regular productive, day-to-day life was possible.

Fueled by the amazing insights I'd learned at Dr. Jean Houston's "Awakening to Your Life Purpose" course and Dr. Claire Zammit's nine-month program, "Feminine Power Mastery," I was ready to discover what this life had to offer. I listened to many online interviews that inspired me. I discovered Darius M. Barazandeh, founder of You Wealth Revolution, who introduced me to Hans Christian King, a gifted medium of over sixty years and a spiritual teacher. I signed up for a special offer to get a personal reading with him. Hans' voice was so clear, and his message penetrated deeply. He said I needed to get out of my way, learn to quiet my busy mind, and not take myself too seriously. Then, right at the end of the call, without my asking, he said, "You will remarry and you have both shared many lifetimes together. He also has quite a spiritual bit going on."

Wow, this blew me away. I was finally not searching for love and happy to be single rather than being with the wrong person. Also, I did not consider myself spiritual. As excited as this made me feel, I didn't share this information with anyone in my family, as I would have to admit I had seen a medium. There was some sense of shame that I would trust such a source or even need guidance. Still, the news made me smile, and I just put it to the back of my mind. Even if it did not turn out to be accurate, it made me feel good. Interestingly, Hans had written a book, *Guided*, which was how I felt for the first time.

About this time, I also discovered Diana Cooper, who had helped countless people find their life mission and empower their lives. I saw her speak at the Mind Body Spirit Festival in London and decided to join her on a trip to Egypt for the auspicious 11/11/11 date. It felt like a great time to be somewhere special in the world and, even more exciting, my younger daughter agreed to come with me. Our group had exclusive access to the Karnak Temple and we were there at exactly eleven minutes past eleven a.m. on 11 November 2011. It was a memorable experience, and we could return after dark to see the magnificent ancient site with its colossal columns and obelisks lit up. I had seen many pictures of orbs before, but on this trip, for the first time, the photographs I took had so many orbs it looked like it was snowing. It was awe-inspiring to see what our ancient ancestors had created. I felt this same awe and wonder when I visited Machu Picchu in Peru. How could we even consider these people less evolved than us? My brother is a civil engineer; he said we would be hard-pressed today, even with all our modern equipment and technology, to recreate these wonders with the same precision.

I finally completed my teacher training qualification after finding a London-based "Body Control Pilates" studio when I moved back to England. It had involved many weekends and months traveling by train into London, attending training, and doing exams, so this felt like a significant achievement. With no idea how I would ever find time to teach, since my work kept me traveling abroad without a fixed schedule, I seemed to be preparing for an unseen future when I would have other income options.

I for the first time felt able to let go of self-doubt, fear, betrayal, overthinking, and shame, to replace them with forgiveness, confidence, love, trust, joy, freedom and self-care.

I decided that my life purpose was to give and receive love. I realized that self-love was a critical starting point. At the end of my life, I wanted to answer the question,""Did I love enough?" with a resounding YES! Learning to be happy with myself, independent of what I had or did, was a big challenge but necessary to find happiness anywhere.

We are conditioned from an early age to consider being selfish as bad. It is clear that while sharing is good, there is a need to be "selfish" regarding self-care and self-love. When we fly on a plane, we are instructed during the safety demonstration to fit our oxygen masks first before trying to help others. Here we easily understand we are of little use to anyone else if we can't breathe but don't easily remember this in other situations. Taking responsibility for our happiness can free our loved ones to explore their own lives without feeling tied and indebted to us."

> *"The day will come when, after harnessing space, the winds, the tides, and gravitation, we shall harness for God the energies of love. And on that day, for the second time in the history of the world, we shall have discovered fire.""*
>
> ~ Pierre Teilhard de Chardin

How much effort does it take to hold onto something you think you need?

When did you last do something for your enjoyment without feeling any guilt?

Do you treat yourself like your very best friend?

CHAPTER 17

CONNECTED

*"For it was not into my ear you whispered but into my heart.
It was not my lips that you kissed but my soul."*

~ Judy Garland

2012

His name is Willis; we meet on the first day and hang out in the same small group of friends we connect with, enjoying most meals and sessions together. On the second day, during a lunch break, we walk along the beach together. The air is cold and crisp, the sea crystal clear, and the beach sands sparkle in the bright sunshine. Celebrated as Monterey Peninsul"s""Refuge by the Sea"" Asilomar State Beach is breathtakingly gorgeous. He asks my surname, and while this is quite a simple question I have to consider my reply. I have been divorced for thirteen years but still use my married name. Changing it just seemed too complicated and too much effort, and it felt less complicated, having the same surname as my children.

He responds, without hesitation,""Oh good, then you will have no issue changing it""

I do not react; there is too much implied. I could be hearing what I want to hear. On the third day, there is a moment between us, and I say "" I see you"" I had never said that to anyone before. I remember the African Zulu word of greeting, "Sawubona," which means precisely this. He does not say so but thinks I'm using a cheap line from the movie, *Avatar*, that I have yet to see.

We kissed for the first time as we welcomed the new year, 2012. We enjoyed a fantastic night of dancing and celebration and finally parted to go to bed, agreeing he would try changing his return flight to the 2nd of January, the same day as mine. We could then spend at least twenty-four hours together. I had to return to work and could not change my flight home. I was staying in a twin room, and my roommate left at the close of the retreat, so we were sorted for his extra night's accommodation. We had a quiet space to figure out if we could see each other again; this was not a conventional holiday romance. He lived in Texas, and I lived in England; this was unbelievable!

He moved his bags to my room, and we crashed, exhausted by four full days of retreat, meeting amazing people and the authors who had inspired us both to be there. Hoping to recuperate before dinner, we rested in each other's arms and slept soundly. We had befriended a lovely couple who were also staying an additional night and made plans to enjoy an evening at a local restaurant together. Explaining what happened next is tricky since I needed help understanding it myself. We both woke in an altered state that Willis recognized as *satori*. In the Zen Buddhist tradition, satori refers to the experience of awakening to one's true nature. I was not only in the world but also everything in it! Suddenly without warning, all boundaries and distinctions disappeared. The line between me and any other was no more. I experienced separation as an illusion, and this expanded state felt extraordinary. Feeling integral to the nature of existence was a profound realization.

I'd had no experience with hard drugs, but felt it felt like somebody might describe a psychedelic trip. When the world returned to some separation, I was no longer the same self I was before. I felt like I was floating on a cloud. I was laughing without reason, dancing for joy. I refer to this as "my oneness experience." I still can't quite understand what happened, let alone express it in words. I was only sure that this incredible experience changed me, my life had changed, and the man that I met and connected with, was the trigger. Even if I had no idea what the relationship would look like, I knew, beyond any shadow of a doubt, that we would be together for the rest of our lives.

We went to dinner that night like we were high, laughing and crying as we tried to understand what had happened to us. I giggled and told him the last thing my father said before I left: "Just don't bring home an American!" We said goodbye the next day. After watching him board his plane to Houston, I sat there, waiting for my flight back to London and feeling like it may all have been a wonderful dream.

As I flew home, I wrote this in my journal:

What does it feel like to be in the flow? I am floating in this world but somehow feel out of it. I am in a plane flying high above the Earth, and it is impossible to sense our speed. I try to figure out the time, my home time, the current time in the air, or the time I started. I can't connect to what is real. My senses are in hyperdrive. My meal arrives, and there is nothing plain or simple about this food; everything tastes spectacular. A simple macaroni cheese meal is mind-blowing, just like being in a five-star restaurant! Relating to where I am isn't easy, nor can I connect with who I am. All previous identities and associations seemed to have faded and no longer make sense. The world in which my mind was the master driver appears disconnected. So, who am I if I am no longer this cacophony of mind chatter? Still firing on all cylinders, super alive, vibrant, and full of life, but oneness can't be described as flow as there is no other and nowhere to go.

We emailed and skyped every day. On the 8th of January, I wrote in my journal:

> *I don't remember him asking me to marry him, maybe because we both know there is no question. My mind is quiet; I am missing my usual worries of "what-ifs" and warnings; this is strange enough to be significant. It confirms to me this whirlwind decision is correct. I have never felt so secure and sure about anything before.*

On the 28th of January 2012 – exactly one month from the day we first met – Willis flew to join me in England. I collected him from the airport, and we said our private marriage vows at a local abbey ruin on the way home! It felt important that we started our relationship from this place of deep commitment and did not need any audience or outside approval. It was icy cold, the air crisp, and the grass crunched underfoot as we walked. He was exhausted after a long flight, woefully underdressed for the English winter, and still had much to learn about this country.

I was still working, and he spent his days trying to find his feet in this foreign land. We did manage a small mini-honeymoon in Switzerland, bolted onto the end of a business trip. We spent the time getting to know each other from the outside, as normal couples do. Our relationship so far seemed precisely the opposite, as it had been from the inside out: I felt I knew him, and he knew me, at a soul level, but we had so much to learn about the regular details of our lives! In fact, I didn't even know anything of the path that had brought him to the retreat. I thought about all the various parameters required by any conventional dating site: the age of the man you're looking for; his income bracket and level of education, the maximum radius he should live from you. Had I answered any of these questions, I would have missed him.

We can best describe our relationship as "effortless belonging" – meaning it was clear that we belonged together and were free to show up fully, without any pretense or façade to impress each other. We felt guided every step of the way; this is not something either of us could have knowingly orchestrated.

We spent many nights planning and figuring out how to join our physical lives together. On the 1st of April, he flew back home to sell his house and car and sort out all his belongings. He even had to find good homes for his beloved cat and dog. Luckily he had already started to close his business before we met, as he intended to move to a community in Northern California. Have you read Elizabeth Gilbert's book, *Committed*, where she describes the nightmare of residency visas? If so, you have an idea of our experience. Never assume that two people from first-world countries can fall in love and decide to live together! Everything was complicated, and it was an uphill battle. Quite apart from the cost, I wondered how people less tech-savvy than us could even manage the application process.

We had decided to have a formal wedding to include all our friends and family and make our sudden union feel a little more stable and conventional. I know my father breathed a sigh of relief, knowing this was serious and not just a passing infatuation or mad holiday romance.

I finally had my opportunity to plan the wedding I had always dreamed of. We paid for it ourselves and did not need to ask my father for support, as I had to for my first wedding. I even got to design my wedding dress! I chose not to have a white wedding but enjoyed choosing a silver dress to match my hair, which showed signs of grey.

Finally, Willis made it back from America on the 16th of May, and we were married on the 16th of June. He jokingly referred to us now as a genuine "African American" couple. There was not a single moment of question or doubt, just the logistical challenge of consolidating our lives with an ocean that divided our families and possessions. It was sad that we could not gather all our children for our wedding, but as they were in America and Australia it seemed ridiculous. I share this note my daughter in Australia wrote, as it always brings a tear to my eye when I read it.

The Future

To my dear mother and her new husband, Willis,

As I look into your future, I see you both in a house and a garden filled with trees. I see dinner parties surrounded by friends and a vegetable patch you love to tend. I see cozy nights in front of the fire, your kitchen as the heart of your home, and a Victorian bath brimming with foam. You sat by the window watching the snow, reading papers, and learning to grow. I see pictures of family in quirky frames, laughter, pain, kisses, and tears, and you help each other confront your fears. I see Willis as your best friend and lover, and I want to thank you, Mother, for all you are and all you have done; I am glad that now you get to be the one. Although there are great oceans that keep us apart, know that you are always in my heart. The three musketeers, as once we were known, I am happy to say, we have now grown. I wish I were with you on your special day, but as I am not, just let me say I wish you all the happiness in the world and all the love I can send.

Yours forever, your daughter and friend.

How long had I dreamed of this relationship? How hard had I tried to find this perfect match to share my life? My miracle happened when I decided I would rather be alone than waste my life with anyone who held me back and stopped me from showing up fully without hiding. First, I had to stand firm, rooted in integrity, honesty, and self-worth.

By some miracle, quite suddenly, I was no longer alone and had a newfound sense of belonging that had nothing to do with where I lived. Even more significant than this, if it is possible to imagine, I now felt the presence of an invisible helping hand guiding me beyond my wildest dreams.

Whatever your dreams or desires, you can attract them to you. When the space and intention are clear, we start resonating or pulsing a signal that almost acts like a vacuum. Have faith in unseen forces and the universal laws of nature. As we search for something or someone to share our lives with, we may discover that it is not about filling a gap but rather the vast potential that lies in deep, lasting relationships.

The best way to start clearing and making space is to recognize and dismantle some negative beliefs you may have collected on your journey. What we appreciate appreciates, so we must love who we are and magnify our gratitude for all we already have. Also, there is value in contemplating all your past romantic relationships – the good, the bad, and the ugly. Some relationships can just remind us how far we have come, while others we might be sad to have lost. Remember where you were at the time and what you believed about yourself.

I had read, and learned much from, Katherine Woodward Thomas's book, *Calling in "The One"*, – including the importance of clearing your physical space as well as mental debris. Sure enough, I did not have a single empty drawer or shelf in my wardrobe! I immediately emptied a bedside drawer. Focus on how you would like to feel in this new relationship and try to let go of other expectations that might block your needs.

Not everyone needs or wants a partner with whom to travel through life. If this is true for you, the good news is you only need to take care of yourself and enjoy the journey of discovering what lights you up to move on with passion.

> *"Your task is not to seek for love, but merely to seek and find all the barriers within yourself that you have built against it."*
>
> ~ Rumi

Are you willing to release old beliefs that no longer serve you?

Have you considered the most important relationship as the one you have with yourself?

Is your vision of a perfect relationship one you created new or one unconsciously inherited?

CHAPTER 18

THE GREAT AWAKENING

*"The thirst to be boundless is not created by you;
it is just life longing for itself."*

~ Sadhguru

2013

I am all dressed in white, sat cross-legged on the floor, surrounded by at least a thousand others. Everyone looks far more comfortable than I feel. Sadhguru sits on a platform no more than a hundred feet from us. He seems to have an eagle eye for socks, and for some reason, they are not allowed! We join in the invocation. I have never felt the vibration of this many *AUMs* resonating together. The initiation begins, all eyes closed. The air around me crackles with energy. At some point, I feel a considerable vibration, like the floor beneath me is moving. Could this be an elaborate special effect? I am still quite skeptical. I'm dying to look around, but not brave enough to open my eyes. I somehow relax into the experience and have no idea how much time passes before I hear Sadhguru's voice from afar, saying, "Now gently, very gently, open your eyes."

I never imagined myself in this situation; this is a scene from someone else's movie. I don't even know what a guru is other than referring to someone accomplished in their field! Yet here I am.

Willis and I began our honeymoon in Barcelona which presented me with the opportunity to have dinner with a dear friend and colleague at her home. We had met while working in South Africa, and our paths crossed again in England and Switzerland; now, I was in the London office and she was serving as the Chief Financial Officer of the company's Spain organization. We both had girls of a similar age. It was great to catch up and introduce her to my new husband. They got on like a house on fire, and he immediately recognized a picture she had framed of Maharishi Mahesh Yogi, who played a significant role in his life. We had never spoken about her faith in all the years of working together. I was simply in awe of the exquisite Indian saris she would wear to work every Friday. We enjoyed a magnificent home-cooked Indian dinner together, with food that was vibrant in color and brought my every tastebud to life. It made my home cooking feel very dull and bland in comparison. Touching other cultures brings me so much joy.

Six months later, she wrote to tell me of a fantastic opportunity in which she thought we might be interested. Her guru, Jaggi Vasudev (Sadhguru), was coming to London, and it was such a fantastic event that she planned to fly from Spain for the weekend to attend. First, we had to complete the Isha 'Inner Engineering' online training. I can honestly say if I had done nothing more than this one online training, my life would have changed. It was like finally receiving the user's manual for living in this body, finding the controls, and learning to navigate my life.

There would still be hundreds of people in London, but nothing like the thousands attending if he did the same program in India. Why not?

It seemed like it would at least be an incredible experience. We made the decision and signed up to join the in-person initiation gathering.

The timing must have been perfect for me; by then, I was not surprised; I got drawn, one step at a time, into a new life of daily practice and greater purpose. I now trusted being an inextricable part of the great mechanism of life.

What is a guru, and why are they needed anyway? Sadhguru jokingly refers to himself as a GPS (Guru Positioning System). While a GPS is not essential, it is a valuable navigation tool, especially if traveling somewhere new. You need to know where you want to go; it helps you see where you are, and then you have to move before you start getting directions. *Gu* means darkness, *Ru* means dispeller, so the Guru is literally "lighting your way."

I love that Sadhguru said the only advice he ever gave his daughter was *never to look up or down on anyone or anything*. Such a clear message that we are neither better nor worse than anyone. We like to think of ourselves as intellectuals but often don't recognize that how we think creates how we feel and leaves us at the mercy of our emotions. From this emotional state, we distort our vision and create identities and attachments that limit the truth of who we are, being embodied fully.

We might earn the most valuable wisdom by admitting what we *don't* know. Faith and atheism are both based on belief: our ability to stay open without coming to conclusions will ensure a lifetime of discovery as they anchor us into one position. While it can feel safe, it prevents us from the ultimate freedom to explore and live fully.

The mind, by its nature, creates a need to know, and it is very good at dissecting information to help us understand things. Yet, clearly seeing and understanding the parts of anything does not allow us to know the essence of its entirety. You may choose to practice the ancient art of yoga or qigong, however, we also have modern tools like the HeartMath Institute created to help us access a state of coherence, or alignment, among the heart, mind, emotions, and physical systems. Learning to activate qualities of the heart, such as loving-kindness, can have considerable benefits in our lives and those around us.

My curiosity about what I could neither see nor touch, but sensed, began to grow. We all talk about a gut feeling or being "called" to do something, maybe without understanding the source of that guidance. Though, like most people, I had some concept of our sixth sense, I had never tried to understand it. I am sure, though quite super, there is nothing abnormal about this extra sense. While I might be clairsentient (clear feeling), clairaudient (psychic or telepathic hearing) and claircognizant (clear knowing) are beyond my current experience. James Lovelock's Gaia Hypothesis was more than just a theory of a living planet but a synergistic, interdependent complex system of which we are an integral part. We talk about the protection and preservation of nature without getting that *we are nature*; it is not separate from us at all. I marveled at how birds that migrated from South Africa to Europe could know when to delay their departure if the weather was not yet suitable for their return. They seem to have access to an internal system more accurate than our sophisticated global weather satellites! I also discovered a wonderful lady, Ana-La-Rai, who is a clear voice and channel for The Alchemy Collective Consciousness. She facilitates a free weekly meditation gathering that co-creates with participants in divine service, to support the transition of the planet and its people, with vibrational infusions of love and light. Do I know any of this to be true? Of course, I can't say for sure, but I loved the idea of doing something that could remotely help our precious planet.

As Anthony De Mello discusses in his book *Awareness*, we don't realize we have been sleepwalking; we need to wake up and not let our happiness depend on our preferences. Religions and morality both give us boundaries of right and wrong, much like a child in a playpen. If we can expand our conscious awareness to the point where loving-kindness is our predominant nature, then boundaries are no longer necessary. Much like children, we still need guidance from outside before we develop the wisdom to "do no harm" as we discover the boundless infinity within that expands to the limitless expanse of existence itself.

It is fun to share my current perspective for our collective, looking at our relationship to everything from the secure place of not knowing the truth of anything.

> *"When we are no longer able to change a situation,*
> *we are challenged to change ourselves."*
>
> ~ Victor Frankl

Are you aware of conclusions you have made that prevent you from exploring further?

When you connect with someone else do you recognize that you are also connecting to yourself?

Have you ever had an experience that changed how you relate to the world?

CHAPTER 19

PURPOSE

"Life isn't about finding yourself. Life is about creating yourself."

~ George Bernard Shaw

2018

I am excited about the call with Hans. I had planned to wait until my career was over and get his input when I needed it most, but I'm feeling so restless now. So many questions. My father's hallucinations and suffering, concerns about planning a big family wedding for my daughter, and the fear of what to do next if I lose my job. The Zoom meeting starts, and I see his kind face on the screen; he immediately asks," How can I serve you, my dear?"

I reply, "I am excited to meet you again; such a wonderful opportunity. I want to know whatever 'comes through' for me, but I also have some pressing questions I would like to ask." I am poised, pen in hand, ready to capture his reply.

He says this is a good period for me; it is a quiet time, without lots happening. Three to four months could open a lot of new doors. It is a time of self-discovery. What do I want to feel and experience? It is a good opportunity to put this awareness together. I will always have enough. Will

I let my mind chatter hold me back? If I lose my job, the company will do me a favor. I need to be concerned about fear; it is my block to be able to serve and make a difference. The next level of discovery will take me to a whole new level; this is a time for change and renewal. It is a time of letting go and learning to trust, I am not alone! I will get through, and all this will pale into insignificance. I should be excited; the best is yet to come!'

I ask the questions I had thought of in advance of this call, which right now seem rather silly and insignificant. Still, Hans answers me with deep compassion and understanding.

I thank him sincerely; we say goodbye, and he is gone. I am somehow disappointed. What did I expect – to be told my future? That, I know, is up to me to create. Still, I take the main message, "The best is yet to come," and smile; I can't wish for more.

Hans sadly passed away less than four months after this meeting. If I had waited to speak to him, as I had initially planned, it would have been too late!

I was excited; my challenge amid this crazy change was to "simply" stay in the present, where there could be no place for fear. I avoided allowing my husband to be my provider; his saying, "It is all good; I have you covered," triggered my fear of dependence. Stop, no; this was an old story; I recognized the pattern. Fierce independence was blocking me from being able to receive. I sat with this awareness; I was safe, powerful, and passionate about life. Hans said, "The time is good for a change," and I felt ready. I knew, maybe for the first time, that I was enough. I had a vision of a baby bird in an egg. For sure, it is enough, but will it reach its potential? It has to be strong enough to listen to the natural urge and fight its way out of the shell to grow. My work had been my excellent protective shell. It was time for me to break free.

I still grappled with the dilemma between doing and being. Maybe this originated as graffiti on a wall somewhere, "To do is to be" – Jean-Paul

Sartre; "To be is to do" – Socrates; "Do be do be do" – Frank Sinatra. I added my version, "Be, do, be." This dilemma always intrigued me, as I considered the great mystics sitting in a cave in a state of bliss without the need to do anything, unlike me in a constant frenetic state, of getting through my never-ending "to-do" list. The trick in solving this dilemma was realizing that being can't be separated from doing. Doing is either driven by need, like eating, drinking, or going to the toilet, or it is an optional activity, things we think we should be doing. My husband thinks "should" is a bad word and he makes me laugh when he says, "Don't should yourself." In the optional category, the busier we get, the less we realize we have a choice. We simply lose the ability to discern clearly and fall prey to what our minds dictate we should be doing. We can consciously decide how we are being within any activity. Whatever I am doing, I can be fully present and choose my state of being. I enjoyed my new affirmation, "In this life I can choose to be happy, or I can choose to be unhappy, so I choose to be happy as it leaves no time for troubles." I quickly discovered this was easier said than done and required constant practice. Doing is the expression of being; for sure, it's not balanced or connected to being in a state of do, do, do. I had focused on doing most of my life. Doing was a means of survival and providing for my family.

I grew up with the story that only the strongest survive; being average is not good enough, and "the devil finds work for idle hands!" What defines work? It qualifies if you're earning a living, building, or working on your home. Painting a wall, yes; painting a picture, no. How deep was this story of mine?

Playing a sport does not count as work, but it is at least generally accepted as a constructive use of time, an effort to keep fit and healthy. If you're sitting, then you are just being lazy. You have to put everything you have into your work. Many other people would be happy to step into your job if you aren't good enough or reliable enough. I was a doer, *par excellence*! I could manage a project within an inch of its life. I could write lists and get things done. Rome might very well have been built in a day if I were the foreman – at least, this is what my ex-husband used to say!

So here I was, within a profound inquiry about what constitutes work and value. I got to decide if I classified something as "work." I got to determine the difference between work and play. Only my relationship with what I was doing made the difference. For some people, there is no distinction between work and play. Would I ever enjoy mopping the floors? I did not know, but I got to choose. Whether you got paid for anything you did was irrelevant if you got some satisfaction from it. Value gets determined by others. They decide if what I did adds value and is worth compensation. However, I should not let that be my sole driver either. What someone else thought about me was none of my business. If Vincent van Gogh had stopped painting when most people did not appreciate him, we would now be without thousands of his masterpieces.

How long had I struggled with the fundamental question, "What is my purpose?" I must have a reason for being. I listened to Marianne Williamson talk about this as a "luxury problem," somewhat irritated that we should think our purpose was unique. If we were struggling to survive, this question would not even arise. I understood it an error to consider that my purpose needed to be my profession; it may be as simple as finding my joy.

Having found my dearly beloved husband and managed to enjoy a successful career, I nevertheless found myself with big questions and insecurities. It was essential to realize that my life would never be smooth, plain sailing without any challenges. The most profound journey I still had was to continue discovering, one by one, the hidden wounds within that could trigger me without warning.

Maybe the truth is that we do not need to find our purpose; it is in each of us, only needing space for expression. We are here to unpack all of the collections built up in our memories, discover our essence, and then be able to see it in others. Once we know our true nature is to be happy and peaceful, there is nothing to "get," and it then becomes an exercise of clearing, to discover what is already there. The mystery of our deep inner purpose seems less important as we find peace with being, irrespective of our doing.

We no longer need to worry if we are good enough and have what it takes to get somewhere or deserve something. It is our life's work to realize our divine nature and let it shine.

During an interview, Oprah shared that, "Our talent can drive our careers and what we choose to get paid for, where our gifts are our calling, and what we were made for!" Live every day "on purpose," in deep gratitude, with love in your heart, and smile. Breathe; how good does that feel?

There is no exam to pass, no right or wrong. There are, for sure, different ways to go about this journey of discovery, and some may be more effective than others. The more we "unpack," the greater clarity we get in experiencing the light as our essence. As it naturally shines brighter, it helps others to see what they are doing too. There is no need to fix anyone else; just shine some light, and the world will look brighter as we all get lighter and lighter. Imagine us like fireflies; as we light the way, we can see better and do what we do best, no longer working in the dark.

"A perfect life smells of bullshit."

~ Amber Fossey, Be Wild, Be Free

Try saying, "I am what I am, and what I am, is enough!" Can you feel the truth and relief in that?

Can you find peace just resting and doing nothing without judging yourself?

What is your heart telling you?

CHAPTER 20

GRACE

*"The winds of grace are always blowing,
but you have to raise the sail."*

~ Sri Ramakrishna

2020

Wow, we did it! The fantastic sound of a champagne cork popping announces a special celebration, and every little bubble of fizz holds our gratitude. We propose a toast to a new chapter in our lives. The two of us have only the couch we sit on and our bed unpacked, ready for our weary bodies when we sleep, as it has been a very long day. Boxes still surround us without a single curtain hung, but the view is spectacular. We are up on a hill; we can see the twinkling lights of the town below and the patchwork of dark where the fields lay, with roads that stitched them together, as the occasional vehicle lights their existence. We sit in silence for some time, taking in the feeling of this sanctuary that is now our home.

I have not been without fear; these last months have allowed this destructive energy to fester in my monkey mind. Indeed, I had received notice of my redundancy when my company decided to move my position to India (deemed a low-cost country) – meaning I was on borrowed time before losing my job. Would we manage without my income, as my husband has already retired and is living on his pension? What will I do next? Then the stress of trying to sell our house and buy a new home. Fear only takes root when I think I should be in control. The art of surrender and trust takes practice. Breaking old patterns and stories of "not enough" is deeply held in the very tissues of my body. It takes constant vigilance to recognize and stop the return of fear, digging past the surface to remember something more constructive to take its place. I breathe deeply to pull myself back into the moment, the only one that counts. I can't change the past; the future is merely my imagination. I sit here now, and all my stupid little worries seem laughable when I witness such perfect timing and grace.

The company I worked for decided to move their premises, about thirty miles from where they were, to central London. They then gave me a work-from-home contract; since I was already serving my six-month notice period, relocating my job was deemed unnecessary. No longer tied to the office, I could consider where we wanted to live. Our current home was in a little village that got busier by the day. The farm, just behind us, inherited by the children when their father died, became the object of subdivision for a proposed housing development – no organic produce was to be found, even in the farm shop! The quiet of country life was calling us, and Willis and I instantly felt at home in Glastonbury while there for a weekend retreat. We found a lovely organic supermarket on the High Street and freedom of expression that lifted our spirits. Glastonbury is now famous for the music festival that started in 1970, the day after Jimi Hedrix died, with less than two thousand attendees. Today, there are thousands of performers and two hundred thousand attendees recorded. Also known as the Isle of Avalon, a land of myth and magic, there is always something going on, even in the depths of winter. With Fairy Fayres, Wytches Markets, Dragon Processions, Beltain Celebrations led by the Green men, and the Goddess Temple, it is no wonder we fell in love with its charm. My husband joked that it was the first place in his life where he felt like a conservative.

We sold our house in January, but it took ages and nerves of steel as we waited for the solicitor to finalize the contract, and dates frequently changed, delaying our search for a new home. Finally, with our house sale agreed upon, we started house hunting in earnest. We had shortlisted a few properties to view over the weekend; we needed the house to feel suitable for us, and each one had something missing. On Friday afternoon, we took a quick last-minute look at the estate agent listings and found one we had not seen before and immediately knew it was perfect for us. We called the agent to put in our offer over the phone, but he refused without us having seen it in person. We booked a viewing the next day and still looked at the other properties, just in case. The moment we parked outside the house, there was no question that we had found our new home. We went directly to the estate agent's office the second we had finished looking around the house, and the sellers accepted our offer; we were thrilled.

I was determined to use my annual leave to move, carried over from the previous year that I would forfeit at the end of March if not taken. I decided to put my foot down, as I reached a "here-to-no further" moment, with the solicitors, who kept pushing out the move date. Finally, we were able to exchange contracts and start the big move. As we packed up our old home, news of COVID was getting more urgent. We planned to eat out and avoid cooking on our last night, but the restaurant suddenly closed. Things were changing fast.

As we sat that first evening in our new home, sipping champagne, we did not know the government had declared a COVID lockdown in England. We still expected the movers to return the following day to complete offloading our household possessions! We were so lucky they decided not to return to base with a truck half full of our furniture, as their company had instructed them to do. Wow, this gave "just in time" a whole new meaning!

I now somehow recognized being in flow, where there again seemed to be evidence of the invisible helping hand, orchestrating perfect timing, far beyond my own thinking mind's ability. These magic moments reminded me that it's all good, that even if the going gets tough and that nasty feeling of fear returns, I am not alone.

The journey from the head to the heart can be long, but grace starts to weave magic in our lives when they work together in balance and flow. As we learn to trust in the greater field of life, the more we feel part of it and no longer separate.

If in doubt that we are an integral part of this magnificent web of life, simply quiet the mind and study a single flower or working bee, to witness the extraordinary nature that goes beyond our imagination. From this still place within, trust in the perfection of all things, even if they seem flawed to our individuated minds. When we can enter a state of wonderment, the truths of existence quietly reveal themselves. Remain curious, and let that curiosity guide you.

Attempting to describe grace is like trying to explain the fragrance of a flower. We may not even notice it if we are busy or have a stuffy nose and cannot smell. We can't use words to describe that which is beyond description.

> *"I do not at all understand the mystery of grace – only that it meets us where we are but does not leave us where it found us."*
>
> ~ Anne Lamott

Do you trust that you are a part of nature and that nature is a part of you?

Have you experienced grace or synchronicity in your life?

Do you take time to smell the roses, observe the little things in life, and practice the art of deep contemplation?

CHAPTER 21

PASSING ON

"She remembered who she was, and the game changed."

~ Lalah Delia

2020

It is the 15th of June, and I am sitting in my home office, shackled to my computer by my headphones. It's been one meeting after another, the last of which is my final notice meeting. I did not know what to expect, but not this! I thought there might be some recognition for my twenty-four years of service, but nothing. The HR lady, who is about twenty-three years old and looks like a Barbie doll, did not go through any details, just said, "Sorry, I know this is a lot to take in." I feel pretty flat. I have to use DHL to ship back all my equipment, and they will process the final payroll today. All done. I feel a little sick to my stomach. Not nice. It feels like someone has flipped a switch within me, and I still need to do the job up until the end of this month.

At last, freedom from the big corporate world, to align what I do with what I care about, seems equally exhilarating and terrifying. I am contemplating this when the phone rings, and I hear my stepsister's voice say, "Dad has just passed away."

I wonder why we say "passed away" instead of "died"? I am relieved; it is not a moment too soon, as I consider his suffering, but it still comes as a huge shock. Being happy with any part of my life while he was in such a dreadful place made me feel guilty. I feel isolated and alone, thanks mainly to COVID rules that keep us in our own homes, forbidden to travel. I am of course, with my wonderful husband, but he is like my other self; we, are in fact, almost like one. It is outside this bubble that I am now looking for love and support. I can't rush to see my daughters, and I can't even hug my brother. I am feeling distraught; I am not sure what has changed, only the world feels very different without my father in it.

Ordinarily, when we experience a significant life event, family and friends congregate to support each other. It was understandable that I wanted to be with those I loved, as I experienced a loss they shared. I needed this connection to get support and help to process the trauma, but this could not happen under lockdown rules. My father's cremation took place in isolation, and there was no funeral to say farewell. I was not sure it even felt real.

My father had endured ten years of excruciating pain due to collapsed discs in his spine, for which he took morphine and other heavy pain meds that may have been instrumental in causing his "Dementia with Lewy bodies." Before his diagnosis, I had never even heard of this type of dementia. I later watched *Robin's Wish,* a documentary about Robin Williams' death, and was surprised to discover he had suffered from the same condition. Of course, there are many nasty diseases, but this one feels particularly cruel. It seems to be Parkinson's and dementia rolled into one, so you lose your cognitive ability and your body fails too. If your mind goes, let it be a one-way street; in other words, if I cannot remember, I cannot remember, period. No, this nasty beast seems to flicker on and off, from one moment, with terrifying hallucinations, to the next with a clear mind. These moments of clarity meant he could still discuss what he saw and how real it seemed, and he would apologize to those around him. When he saw a giant spider next to my face, was it more cruel to deny its existence or move to "safety" to help him cope?

We had visited him on his 81st birthday, on the 3rd of March, just before we moved into our new house, before lockdown, and he said he was looking forward to visiting us soon. Most importantly, I got to say, "I love you," as that was the last time I saw him. We always know when we are doing something for the first time, but not always the last!

I have a photograph of my father taken when I was a little girl, about four years old, and it is my favorite; I am sitting beside him, smiling and looking up at him, and there seemed such deep love between us. Right in the beginning, where there is just a father and a daughter without expectation or disappointment, he was perfect in my eyes, and I in his.

I remember him saying, "Daddy loves triers," a wonderful message to receive as I grew up. I do not recall his handwriting; he never even wrote on cards, and my mother did all the writing. This may be why I treasure that handwritten christening letter from my grandfather. I was grateful my father did enjoy using his Super 8mm motion picture camera, which captured many family holidays and special occasions. Still, I looked around, trying to see him in the things he built and left behind. My dad was a cheery guy everyone liked to be with, he had a considerable presence, and his energy filled the room. I felt this now hollow space inside and out.

In this strange place, where I found myself suddenly without a father, I thought about what I missed. He was the fittest, healthiest person I knew. When he retired, he built an oceangoing catamaran and with his own hands, crafted all the magnificent interior carpentry in cherry wood. To this day, the smell of that wood takes me back to those years of boat-building. As if that was not a big enough challenge, he sailed it from South Africa to England, no small feat for sure. He was active, played veteran league squash in his seventies, and did his morning run to get the daily newspaper. Accidents happen, of course, but I never thought for a second that he would end his life in the way he did. I wish I had taken more time to talk to him about his family and his life experience.

Why does it take a death or an illness to make us contemplate life? We like to think or pretend we will live forever. We do not know when we will die; maybe if we ignore it and do not talk about it, we need not face reality until we are there. It is vastly different from other countries in the world. There are cultures where death is more a part of life. When someone dies, the family sits with the deceased, and children are not protected from witnessing death, like I was. My grandparents died in England, far away from me, and I was an adult with a child of my own before my stepfather died of liver cancer. One day, I listened to a radio program, and they were talking to someone from an end-of-life support charity. When asked who qualified for support, the lady replied, "Anyone with a terminal condition." That made me smile – we are all eligible since life is, by definition, a terminal condition, and the death rate is 100%. Jokes aside, why do we need to get our end date clear or lose someone we love to start living fully?

I still drove to push forward into the unknown past. I had read that life is lived forward but can only be understood by looking backward. I tried to piece together my family tree, and I asked my mother the full names and dates of my grandparents; she said, "Oh dear, why are you doing a family tree? We come from a long line of undistinguished people." I found that sad and questioned why, being distinguished, made any difference.

Ultimately, it is a list of names that took considerable time to discover the details and get them all with the correct dates and connections; I even questioned if it was worth the effort. I found it flat and even a little depressing to see so many lives reduced to just a few strokes of a pen on the page. It reminded me of a poem called "The Dash" by Linda Ellis, about how all that occurs in our lives is represented by that punctuation mark between the dates of our birth and death.

I considered going through the history of their lives and seeing how long they each lived. Whatever you learn from your family history could somehow define your expectations if you are not careful. What if they all died young? Do you subconsciously set this as your life expectancy? As I read names from the past, I could dig up a few precious photographs that captured a moment. Wedding pictures are great; here we got all the family together, dressed up in their best. How hard were their lives? Were they happy and content or stressed and exhausted? Like most lives, it was neither all one nor the other. Being with those you love seems to be essential. Where and how you live seem secondary; each life on the page is a story. How they grew up, learned, and made their way in life. How they found or lost love, had children, and worked to make a living. How they lived is one question, but I also wondered how they died and, most importantly, were they at peace and fulfilled? So, each dash between two dates is a life. We dream, make plans, and strive to meet the goals we set for ourselves.

What if we were all born with a label with a manufacture date, best before, and end date? The manufacture date is simple for most of us. I knew many Africans who did not know their birth date or age; I found this difficult to comprehend. Imagine, rather than knowing all these dates, knowing none of them! How much do we alter how we live based on our age? At each stage in life, we have preconceived ideas about how we should be. What if we did not know how old we were? Our grey hair and inability to jump from a deep squat would tell us we are no longer in our youth. We might rely on comparison with others, which could be inaccurate too. Many think having children later in life keeps you younger. Someone at eighty can look much older than someone at ninety, so much depends on our health. There is a physical age but also a mental age. As we grow up, we all know about the age difference in maturity between girls and boys. Have you heard it said, "A man is a boy and a child forever" or "The difference between a man and a boy is the price of his toys"? It is just fun to contemplate, but our chronological age does not count for everything.

How about knowing your "best before" date? Well, best for what?

My stepfather always said, "Live your life like you're going to die tomorrow and plan your life as though you will live forever"; this always frustrated me. I quickly jumped to the technicalities of a limited bank balance and could not see how to hold both concepts simultaneously. It might be most helpful to know our expiry date. If we knew how long we would live, it would make planning much more straightforward. Still contemplating this possibility, I think I would rather not know. Would you like to know your end date? My mother said the great news is that at her age, she no longer needs to read the information on the long-term side effects of the medication she takes! You get to an age where you no longer buy green bananas.

Getting to know something about my ancestors, what shaped their lives, and questioning their relevance to my life, felt essential. Was this an attempt to expose the game of life? Discovering where I came from gave me a frame of reference. My grandparents lived in quite a different world from me and created a map for future generations. Grandchildren should interview their grandparents; they get far more story and detail than parents ever tell their children. As evolving beings, we are born to be better than our parents, and they have difficulty being fully open and honest with us while they are still trying to set themselves up as the best role models they can be. I do not have any grandparents now, so it might have to be up to my children to interview my mother as their one and only grandparent. My grandchildren will have this book from me as a snail trail of a forgotten past.

My mother is an avid reader; as a child, she would go to the library on her way home from school and get two books; if she were quick, she could read them and then return to get two new ones before they closed that day. She could author a brilliant book, I begged her to, and the answer I got was this: "I might write one day when I'm no longer able to do anything else!" I still feel some trepidation if I imagine her reading this book.

We make nests like birds to protect ourselves from the elements and raise our young.

In South Africa, there are lots of weaver birds. Just like the common sparrow in size, the males have beautiful yellow plumage and a distinct black patch of feathers across their face that inspired them to be aptly named the "Southern Masked Weaver." They make very distinctive woven nests that look like small baskets hanging from a single branch with a tunnel entrance. The male birds have all the color and beauty to show off and attract their mates. For these little weaverbirds, building a nest is the male's job. I loved watching them working hard, day after day. You would be amazed to watch them hanging upside down, so cleverly weaving the grass into a beautiful nest, but this, my friend, is not the end of the story. At the end of the build, the big day comes when he has to find the courage and call his lady love to do the final inspection. Sometimes, in less than a minute, these fussy little female birds, without even looking around entirely, decide it is not up to standard. They immediately start stripping the nest apart. It is pretty upsetting to watch, as the poor male has to start all over again!

Oh, wouldn't it be wonderful if we could understand the birds? I wonder what we would hear. One morning, it was wet and cold as I was getting into my car to drive to work, and the birds were still singing beautifully. I marveled at their happy song, despite the weather. Then as I drove, I considered that they might not be singing for joy. It may just sound like a happy song to me. Was there a vast complaint going on amongst the group? How would I know?

Like birds, we also nest, and I wondered if anyone ever moves into a new home without immediately making changes. It seems natural, wanting to make a home yours by making personal touches and adding your unique stamp. I have looked at pictures in magazines and books to get inspiration and ideas on home decoration. Somehow, as hard as I tried, it looked different from the glossy images when I added everything we owned. It was never possible to start from scratch and buy everything new. Lucky for me I love patchwork quilts; a home that gets decorated organically from different parts is able to tell a story of those that live there. Still, the most important thing is feeling comfortable and at home in your space. How do you feel, in your home?

Clutter is my nemesis; keeping stuff from building up on any flat surface takes continuous effort. If things are uncluttered, I feel good; it gives me space to breathe and move. Is a cluttered space a sign of a cluttered mind? If we are lucky enough, we have a home with a garden. Being close to living things and nature is vital for me. A garden may be unnecessary if you can access a park or open area to walk.

You can put pot plants on a small balcony or grow herbs on your kitchen windowsill.

Gardens also take on a unique shape, depending on the time and effort we dedicate to them. I am in awe of the tenacity of plants. It seems to be if I leave the garden unattended for a moment, it reverts to nature. Grass grows where I do not want it and does not grow where I want it; weeds thrive while a beautiful new shrub decides it cannot survive without care! So complicated, just like us. One plant wants good drainage and other acid soil; prune this one, not that one. I guess it is just learning the art of letting go enough to see what thrives, with the care we can give and control just sufficiently to find a space that provides us joy. The trees grow, like family trees, and continually branch out to reach for light and air. Every leaf and flower is different, but overall, it is a beautiful picture. Humans are not separate from nature; we are unique in color, fragrance, and variety. Some of us are like branches, not leaves or flowers, but no one is better or more important than another. It is only together that we can show our true magnificence. We seldom stop to appreciate the extensive roots of any plant and contemplate how vital they are to what we see growing. Maybe our roots are our energetic bodies, not visible to the naked eye but just as vital to our connection with all that is and the physical body we see.

Our life, like seasons of the year, has phases
time for play, time for learning, time for finding our way in the world, time for love, and time for reflection.

When we each get to the end, whenever it may be, how will we decide if it was a life well lived? Is it as simple as not harming others? Maybe not, but it is a good starting point. For me, the ideal would be adding something valuable to the world. Being a happy, self-fulfilled person and ensuring I am not part of the problem would be a good foundation. Does it make any difference if we focus on expanding our consciousness, joy, and abundance and try to inspire others to do the same? Michael B. Beckwith said he used to speak about "living in joyful anticipation." Now he talks about "living in joyful participation," as we participate in the flow of life.

Death is guaranteed for all of us; it is only a question of how and when we will die. We would all choose to leave without experiencing pain or suffering, but is the sorrow mostly for the loved ones left behind? Who feels the most significant loss? It has not only to do with blood relations and more to do with genuine relationships. When someone's presence has no significant value to you, their absence also has less impact on your life.

We all have experience living in the shadows. Our lives are stories woven from the good, the bad, and the ugly, but by clearing a path through the illusions and gaining perspective, we can look back and see how it all worked together, forming a cobbled picture that may not seem perfect but is beautiful all the same.

> *"Don't be dead serious. Life is a brief sparkle, but you shall be dead for a very long time."*
>
> ~ Sadhguru

What makes a life worth living or a life lived well?

What are your major life choices: moving to a foreign country; getting married; having children; choosing a university, or leaving home?

Are you reacting to life or living as part of it?

What would you change if you knew how long you would live?

CHAPTER 22

THE END IS THE BEGINNING

"The purpose of a story is to lead us back to what matters and show us how everything is connected as part of something larger."

~ Mark Nepo

2021–2022

Today, it is official: I am sick and tired of lockdown! I can't go out for a cup of coffee, meet anyone, or even go for a long walk, without worrying about where to find a toilet, as all the facilities are closed! I am listening to the "Morning Cup of Coffee" playlist, the song about the feeling of going crazy is eerily resonant during this enforced COVID solitude. The weather is wet and windy, and I can't even enjoy cooking for friends. I am longing for the sun to shine, I am definitely a solar-powered vehicle desperately in need of a recharge. I am finally free from the constraints of a full-time job and have time to be, but be what, is the question. I have a beautiful home and the man of my dreams, why oh why can't I just relax and be happy with what is? I feel like there is a fire inside me, and it won't let me rest. Still, I feel I am exactly where I am meant to be.

My left shoulder is not moving and is excruciatingly painful. I know this pain well as my right shoulder was frozen back in 2016, and I never imagined I would relive this experience again. Today I am aware of another miracle, like the one back in 2010 when I got the Rickettsia diagnosis. Here I am with this frozen shoulder for the past six months. I finally get the message about letting go and letting flow. I have been living in a state of holding on tightly and trying to control my life. Now I have found Qigong as the missing link and major part of the solution, not just for my shoulder but my entire life. Only because of this pain, rendering me unable to do Pilates or yoga, I responded to a free, five-day, "Energy Detox and Reboot" event invitation that I would otherwise not have given a second glance. It is the range of motion from Pilates combined with the spiritual depth of yoga and the magic is, it adds awareness to play with the energy, that is me. As an active dancer with the force of life, I am a life-force artist! It feels so good to move and feel my vitality improve daily; this energy flow connects the brain's wisdom with the heart's love and the gut's power. I embrace life's ups and downs and lean into challenges with curiosity, openness, and courage, celebrating each moment. The path to mastery is the path to love.

The COVID pandemic has forced many people to slow down. Stay-at-home mandates gave us plenty of time for reflection. Whether we wanted it or not, we now had time to evaluate our lives, what keeps us busy running around vs. what honestly adds value.

I know not to take good health for granted, but this global pandemic has still impacted beyond what I had imagined; seeing entire cities empty felt like something only to be seen in the movies. As I listened to a documentary about saving our soil on the planet, one sentence landed so loudly for me as evidence of the abundance of nature. "Plant one seed, and it will give you hundreds of seeds." So obvious but mind-blowing when you think about the enormity of that; only death is still. We should not try to save life but live it fully.

My Qigong practice led me directly to the possibility of getting my certification to be a life coach. Looking back at my life I had always been coaching, but simply as part of my job or role as a mother and friend. My last official job title was "Workforce Continuous Improvement Manager" for global IT, to design capability development programs and training to drive workforce effectiveness. Working with colleagues worldwide was fantastic, and I learned so much about our cultural differences and what we all had in common. I had previously pushed away from the concept of coaching because if I needed to teach anyone about life, I would have first to master my own. I finally found a robust system with solid processes and tools that could help anyone. It was all about finding the freedom to get back in the driver's seat of your life and create it consciously. This evolved into relationship coaching, as I understood relationships to be the major driver of our life experiences. Everything along the way had come in perfect timing to get me to this precise point.

The daily world news highlighted many dire situations, so I decided it was critical to lighten up and not take everything too seriously. It was as important to laugh and enjoy life. There is always something to make me smile. Recently we bought a little garden shed, not much bigger than the width of a standard door, to store the washing line and a few garden tools. It came as a flat pack of wooden bits with assembly instructions. My father used to say that there is no such thing as an easy job and this was no exception. Floor and walls in place, it seemed we needed the door to be in and closed to get it squared before screwing in the corner supports from the inside. My husband is nearly six feet tall and had precious little room to move inside, with every movement shifting the walls. We had the bright idea of using ratchet straps to wrap and temporarily secure the outside. It worked like a charm, except when my husband asked me to release the catches, I did not have the hand strength to do it. Okay, I promise I was trying desperately, but it was hopeless. As the severity of our self-made predicament became apparent, the strong words directing my efforts from inside the shed got more urgent. Now, this was not the right time to laugh, but there are certain situations where it seems impossible not to. Has this ever happened to you when a situation requires you to be calm and caring, but you find yourself in fits of laughter? There was a funny side to talking to my husband in a wooden box, like a standing coffin without a lid. I tried cutting the strap, but it was made of super-strength nylon, making it impossible.

I considered tipping it over so he could crawl out the top, but that would not have been possible without injuring him and destroying the shed! Eventually, I pulled myself together and unpicked the stitching on the ratchet buckle strap. I can recall many such occasions where I laughed and not at the most appropriate times. A hearty laugh feels good, and I am sure it is therapeutic. Laughter is the best medicine. I also have found that it is these silly things in life that we all reminisce about when we get together, remembering the things that did not go to plan. Never do we take time to talk about things that went right.

What a world we live in with

crime, discrimination, racism, depression, family disintegration, and social unrest; this list could go on. Discontent and lack of meaning are commonplace, where our old stories no longer work and our beliefs no longer serve us. How do we face cultural confusion and lack of purpose? We cite these as being top issues for teenagers in our time.

I am optimistic by nature and trust the constant breakdown and rebirth in all cycles, but I understand the enormity of our challenges today. I read about these issues that teenagers are facing and realized while I could not fill the gap or solve the problem, I knew how some of these had touched my life and felt sure most of us could relate to them too.

Looking at the world stage can feel overwhelming, and even understanding our physical bodies seems challenging enough. Reading Bill Bryson's book *The Body* is a fantastic way to take a whirlwind tour, and I learned a great deal.

DNA is a curious thing that I do not pretend to understand, but I like to imagine it as being like our building plan. Bruce Lipton did a terrific job of explaining it in a way I could comprehend. Like any design, much changes between the architect's plan and the completed project. Continuing with the building plan analogy, who will build the house, how skilled are they, and what is the quality of the building materials? What if I get involved and decide not to work to plan in a particular area? Can I change the plan itself? Is it possible that I can alter my DNA? I do not have to know, but I still find myself comfortable understanding that while my DNA may well point my direction, it does not dictate my being.

Think about a fortune teller; how much do you believe what they tell you? Can you experience something just because you were expecting it? Is any future, no matter how clear, just a possibility? I like the romantic comedy *Sliding Doors* (1998), because it made me deeply consider multiple storylines in this case, one storyline where the main character catches the train and the other where she misses it. Would the significant events in your life still have played out in any of your chosen scenarios, or might your life have been entirely different?

My life is not simply about me; it is about the lives I touch and how I make other people feel. I choose to live today as if I were going to die tomorrow. I also quite suddenly realized that I needed to play full-on in this life, giving it my all as the world needs each and every one of us to do. I had to feel there was a purpose bigger than what I wanted, to make it worthwhile to be vulnerable and show up in the world. Becoming a transformational coach, I realized, was the answer I needed.

> *"I am grateful to live in a trust that now deeply shapes my life."*
>
> ~ Don Marek

How do you choose to live your life?

Has the job or profession you trained for disappeared, or can you see the end in sight?

Are you conscious of writing your own life story, or do you feel like a victim of circumstance?

> *"Always believe that something wonderful is about to happen."*
>
> ~ Dr. Sukhraj Dhillon

This book was not simply a story about "little" me, but the larger view of humanity I have accessed through fear and struggle. We are not ordinary, but extraordinary, and part of the very magic fabric of life.

These are tumultuous times of accelerating change, and we have learned to expect the unexpected. Time seems to be moving so quickly we can see history in the making. We can watch many world documentaries and see the great numbers of Gaia's species that are becoming extinct daily. Humanity is also on what looks like a precipice, and we might well be part of the next mass extinction. We are at the end of the road, but there must be another dimensional map to give us choices to move forward that are new and exciting. The explosion of artificial intelligence leads us to answer the fundamental question of what it means to be human. I prefer to be optimistic and focus on possibilities beyond our current imagination. No one wants to be insignificant, but many don't dare to be unselfconsciously authentic and seen by others. No one wants to be without purpose, but ... from within, we can find hidden possibilities to expand and re-story our lives as part of a much larger story; we have work to get done. We must remember the truth of who we are, this is not the time to play small. What are our heartfelt desires for ourselves, our children, and our children's children? The urgency behind my words and my sense of the importance of this present time has helped me find the courage to write. All my little ego-based worries pale into insignificance, and I feel driven to give my all and play my most significant game to make a difference, however slight. I hope I can inspire you to do the same, even if the destination is unclear. While this idea does not feel familiar or safe, the temptation is great to return to our familiar comforts, no matter how dull or unfulfilling. The mythic hero undertakes a transformational journey. We are no longer limited by where we live or our culture, the internet has connected us in ways that were never before possible. It is the time for remembering what we are capable of and reawakening our human potential.

Sadhguru said, "If you do not do what you cannot do, it is all right. But if you do not do what you can do, your life is a tragedy."

You and I are not alone, but we are better together, and the power of our relationships is what makes our life experience.

The biggest enemy we face is fear and division; let's not confuse equality with sameness. We are as unique and special as each snowflake but made of the same stuff.

Be a bridge, break down walls to find what unites us, and join humanity's team.

As you have taken the time to read this book, we have engaged in a kind of conversation. I am inviting you to go further, revive your vitality, break down old barriers, and breakthrough to new possibilities, or simply connect with other like-minded individuals who light you up.

We are right now, in this present moment, between what was and what is yet to be.

The best is yet to come! Let's make it so.

BIBLIOGRAPHY

– With thanks to those who helped me find my way.

Dr. Cecile Jadin - A Disease called Fatigue
    https://chronicfatiguesyndrome.co.za/cfs/about-the-book/

Evolving Wisdom - Transformative Education
    https://evolvingwisdom.com/

Meet Jean Houston
    https://www.jeanhouston.com/

Barbara Marx Hubbard - written works
    https://en.wikipedia.org/wiki/Barbara_Marx_Hubbard

Sadhguru, Isha Foundation
    https://isha.sadhguru.org/in/en

The Alchemy Collective
    https://www.thealchemycollective.org/

Humanity's Team Worldwide
    https://www.humanitysteam.org/

HeartMath Institute
    https://www.heartmath.org/

Mark Nepo - spiritual writer, poet, philosopher, healing arts teacher, cancer survivor

   https://marknepo.com/

SATORI Method QiGong

   https://satorimethod.com/

ACKNOWLEDGMENTS

Writing this book has been challenging as I had to find the courage to be seen by you. It has been a cathartic experience and helped me recognize that even a short story carries a voice that may help someone else feel less alone. I also feel called to thank those who have assisted me in this regard, and so many others.

Thanks to my family as the small tribe that loves me regardless of my peculiarities. We are not only bound by DNA but enjoy relationships of meaning that have shaped my being in so many ways. You are the foundation of this story.

Gratitude to all the other teachers who have guided my way, and number far too many to name individually.

I want to recognize the invisible team that guides and supports me every moment, not seen or heard but they are a presence I hold dear.

Transcendent Publishing, for being such a professional team that edited and published this as a high-quality book I can be proud of.

Lastly, I send love and gratitude to my beloved husband for seeing who I am with all my flaws and loving me regardless; you gave me the encouragement I needed to step into the unknown confidently. Without your questions, thoughts, and daily guidance, this book would not exist. Your love, kindness, and spiritual depth are my foundation. I am blessed to have found you as we journey on this life adventure together.

Disclaimer: - I do not want this story to offend anyone, known or unknown. It attempts to reflect the facts accurately but is only my lived experience and, therefore, a relative truth.

Other than my personal story, the things I share are not original but simply ideas and soundbites I collected over the years that made an impression on me.

STAY CONNECTED

If you feel inspired to keep in touch, go to:
Lankavatara.com/Newvenation

I would love to hear from you!
Facebook Page: Newvenation

ABOUT THE AUTHOR

Joanne has a diverse background and is passionate about reading, learning, speaking, travel, connection, and self-discovery. She is in awe of the natural world and the forces that shape us. Joy comes from attracting like-minded people into communities that expand collective and individual potential. As a coach, she helps you connect your internal wisdom to life's challenges and find what makes you come alive to feel fulfilled and reenergized.

Born in South Africa to immigrant parents, her life experience is imbued with African cultural perspectives that cast a light for our self-reflection. As a Body Control Pilates teacher and Qigong practitioner, she is devoted to mind-body-soul vitality. As a wife, mother, and grandmother, she is the one others seek out for advice. Having tuned her skills as a Global IT Manager for a Fortune 500 company, Joanne now directs those skills to human potential through coaching, searching for practical and potent ideas for creating a new future for ourselves, our community, and our planet.

www.ingramcontent.com/pod-product-compliance
Lightning Source LLC
LaVergne TN
LVHW010223070526
838199LV00062B/4704